The Disappearing Deaconess

The Disappearing Deaconess

Why the Church
Once Had Deaconesses
And Then Stopped Having Them

BRIAN PATRICK MITCHELL

EREMÍA
PUBLICATIONS

ALEXANDRIA, VIRGINIA

THE DISAPPEARING DEACONESS
Why the Church Once Had Deaconesses and Then Stopped Having Them

Eremía Publications
An Imprint of Pontic Press
P.O. Box 1
Alexandria, VA 22313

www.ponticpress.com

HARDBACK ISBN: 978-0-9910169-7-6
PAPERBACK ISBN: 978-0-9910169-8-3

Library of Congress Control Number: 2021903451

Cover art: Detail of north wall, Basilica of Sant' Apollinare Nuovo, Ravenna, Italy, B. O'Kane / Alamy Stock Photo, used with permission.

10 9 8 7 6 5 4 3 2 1

To Protodeacon Sergius Miller,

whose kind hand and aesthetic sense

brought order and decency to the cathedral.

"Let all things be done decently and in order."

1 Corinthians 14:40

Table of Contents

Preface

History is not tradition. History becomes tradition only when it is handed down. Many things in the Orthodox Church's two-thousand-year history have been handed down to us, but many things also have not been handed down. Deaconesses have not been handed down. They were handed down to parts of the Church for many centuries but ceased to be handed down to any part of the Church many centuries ago.

If deaconesses had been handed down to us, this book would not have been written because it would not have been needed. We would already know what deaconesses are for and how they fit within the Church. Because they have not been handed down, any proposed "revival" of deaconesses raises innumerable questions about the nature and purpose of what would be for all of us a new clerical order. These questions cannot be answered without reference to the Church's historical experience of deaconesses. We cannot assume simplistically that because the Church once had deaconesses, it can and should have them again. We need to know why only parts of the Church had deaconesses and why even those parts stopped having them. This book answers those questions.

The main body of this book is my master's thesis completed in 2017 at the University of Winchester. The thesis made significant contributions to the scholarship on both deacons and deaconesses by analyzing the appearance and disappearance of deaconesses in light of the Church's teaching on male and female and of changes in other Church offices. I had always hoped to have it published as a book, but about the time of its completion, the Patriarchate of Alexandria surprised the Church worldwide by allegedly making "deaconesses" of several women in the Congo. I therefore decided, on the advice of others, to make the thesis immediately available to the public through my personal blog, brianpatrickmitchell.com, and through Academia.edu. In doing so, I all but satisfied the market for the intended book, eliminating any interest a publisher might have in it. Yet there was still a need for a handy volume providing anyone interested with a clear and thorough examination of the issue of deaconesses from a traditional Orthodox perspective, so I decided to publish the book myself.

This book consists of the thesis with a few very minor changes, plus two important appendices that broaden the scope of the book to include both the current issue of deaconesses and the larger issue of male and female as understood by the Orthodox Church.

Appendix B is "A Public Statement on Orthodox Deaconesses by Concerned Clergy and Laity," signed by fifty-seven Orthodox clergymen and lay leaders and released January 15, 2018. This statement was drafted by me with Fr. Alexander F.C. Webster and Fr. Peter Heers as a response to the Patriarchate of Alexandria's disputed blessing of women for church service in the Congo and to a subsequent public statement in support of these new "deaconesses" issued by several "Orthodox liturgists" on October 24, 2017.

Appendix A is the text of my remarks at a conference on "Renewing the Male and Female Diaconate" organized by the St. Phoebe Center for the Deaconess, held in Irvine, California, on October 7, 2017. These remarks go further than both the thesis and the public statement at Appendix B by outlining a theological basis for the distinction of male and female as the key to understanding the natural and economical relationship of the man and the woman, including, among many other issues, the exclusion of women from clerical orders. A fuller presentation of this "theology of gender" is part of my doctoral dissertation, entitled *Origen's Revenge: The Greek and Hebrew Roots of Christian Thinking on Male and Female*, which will be published later this year by Pickwick Publications, an imprint of Wipf and Stock.

I should also mention that I am currently working on new editions of two other books related to both this book and *Origen's Revenge*:

The first is *The Scandal of Gender: Early Christian Teaching on the Man and the Woman*, published by Regina Orthodox Press in 1998. The research for that book contributed greatly to my master's thesis and doctoral dissertation. It also laid the patristic foundation for the "theology of gender" introduced by me in *St Vladimir's Theological Quarterly* in 2010, summarized briefly but compellingly in Appendix A of this book, and much more fully fleshed out in the last chapter of *Origen's Revenge*.

The second is *Eight Ways to Run the Country: A New and Revealing Look at Left and Right*, published by Praeger in 2006. *Eight Ways* provides an evenhanded analysis of past and present political perspectives in the modern West on the basis of their regard for two fundamental elements of social and political relationships: the recognition of rank and the use of force, represented by the Greek words *archē* and *kratos*. A conceptual refinement of the theoretical basis of *Eight Ways*, adjusting the definition of *archē* from meaning a "recognition of rank" to its patristic meaning as "sourceness" (so to speak), provided the key to the theology of gender suggested by *The Scandal of Gender*, introduced in *St Vladimir's Theological Quarterly*, and developed more fully in *Origen's Revenge*.

I would like to thank my collaborators in drafting the statement at Appendix B, Fr. Alexander and Fr. Peter; the statement's initial signers, especially Fr. Hans Jacobse, who made it possible for hundreds of other faithful Orthodox Christians to add their names; and all those who did so online at Fr, Hans's website, aoiusa.org. Together, by the grace of God, we have met the challenge with lasting effect.

Alexandria, Virginia
Sunday of Orthodoxy
March 21, 2021

Competing Precedents: To Have or to Have Not?

When we hear the word *priest*, many things come to mind. We have met many priests. We know what they look like, what they do, how they act, and how others act toward them. The same cannot be said of *deaconess*. We know deaconesses only through our study of church history, and that history does not tell us much. The image of deaconesses we form in our mind is therefore much less complete and much more imaginary, influenced as least as much by our knowledge of today's male clergy, especially deacons, as by our knowledge of the deaconesses of history. This is true whether we are for or against a revival of the order of deaconess. Both sides imagine deaconesses dressing and acting much like deacons today. Some are alarmed by that prospect; others are thrilled by it.

For those thrilled by it, the case for revival is fairly simple: The Church once had deaconesses; it can therefore have them again. The importance of precedent to proponents of revival is clearly seen in the preponderance of works aimed at proving that deaconesses were once ordained instead of proving a present need for them. Proving a present need is arguably more difficult, given the inherent subjectivity of perceptions of need, but proving a historical precedent for deaconesses is also not without challenges. Precedents depend on similarity: For the deaconesses of old to serve as precedents for deaconesses today, the duties, status, and requirements of one must be substantially similar to the duties, status, and requirements of the other. Otherwise, the ordination of deaconesses today would be not a revival of an ancient order but the innovation of a new order under an ancient and misleading name.

Then there is the problem of multiple precedents: The Fathers of the Church have, in fact, left us not one, not two, but three important precedents regarding deaconesses—a precedent for having them, a precedent for not having them, and a precedent for not having them even after having had them. Much of the ancient Church never had deaconesses. All of the ancient Church that once had deaconesses stopped having them.

No consensus exists on an explanation for any of these precedents. There is general agreement that infant baptism contributed to the disappearance of deaconesses where they once existed, but infant baptism cannot explain their nonappearance elsewhere and is also not thought entirely sufficient to explain their disappearance. Cultural factors are frequently supposed to have played a part by making ancient Christians less tolerant of women in clerical roles, but such suppositions typically assume what no one has shown—that in becoming less tolerant of women in clerical roles, Christians were responding to alien influences and not to a better way within their own tradition as handed down by the Holy Apostles.

Part of the problem is that most research on deaconesses has focused narrowly on ancient texts that mention them. Even when the scope is broadened to include other female "ministries" (widows, virgins, ascetics), the social context necessary for understanding particular gender-coded ministries is missing. Researchers attempt to explain a detail of gender difference without reference to the big picture, which includes not just the surrounding pagan or Jewish culture but also what the Apostles and Fathers taught as Christian truth about the sexes and how early Christians lived out that truth in their daily lives. Such an approach makes anachronism virtually inevitable, especially among younger researchers, whose assumptions about relations between the sexes often differ radically not just from those of ancient Christians but also from those of their own grandparents.

When the big picture is consulted, both the nonappearance and the disappearance of deaconesses are much easier to explain. The Apostles and Fathers taught that the man is the head of the woman, both naturally in the sense of the man's precedence at creation and economically in the sense of the woman's subjection after the Fall. The clerical ranking of women as "deacons" therefore posed a problem from the beginning. The Church minimized the problem either by severely limiting their duties or by not ordaining them. When the few duties assigned to deaconesses were no longer needed, the order survived only as an honor bestowed on nuns, but as the Church's understanding of clerical rank evolved, making women "deacons" made less and less sense, so the Church stopped ordaining them.

This is the theory to be argued hereinafter as a counter to the opinion prevailing among pro-revival researchers, who assume the apostolic institution of the order and therefore a more egalitarian gender order that was only later overcome by cultural forces when church needs changed. The argument that follows will question the apostolic institution of the order and conclude that though church needs did change in ways that lessened the perceived need for deaconesses, the gender order among Christians did not change significantly. As far as can be shown, the only significant change in the gender order among Christians in the period in question was the disappearance of deaconesses, but that disappearance cannot explain itself; it can only be explained by some other change.

As it happens, the church order also changed significantly over time, from a looser, more organic organization in the first century, with many informally recognized ministries and ministers, to a more structured, hierarchic organization with three major clerical ranks and two, three, or four minor clerical ranks (deaconess, subdeacon, reader, and chanter) varying with time and place, as well as a distinction between monastics and non-monastics. This change in the church order made it more and more difficult to maintain a separate ministry for women with the same name as a very different ministry for men.

The argument will begin with a review of what is known and not known about deaconesses before their disappearance, followed by consideration of the factors supposed to have contributed to their disappearance. These factors will be categorized and considered as follows: First, changes in church needs, then changes in the gender order, and finally changes in the church order, with greater attention given to the second and third categories as the more controversial.

As the argument will be made from an Orthodox perspective in an effort to explain why the Orthodox Church stopped ordaining deaconesses, developments in the West after the schism of 1054 will not concern us, neither will the issue of present need among the Orthodox, nor attempts among the Orthodox to revive the order in recent years, nor even the relevance of ancient Christian teaching on gender to Orthodox Christians today. Our only concern is to answer the historical question of the deaconess's appearance, disappearance, and nonappearance. Why did they appear in some places, why did they not appear in other places, and why did they eventually disappear where they had appeared?

These questions have not been answered adequately elsewhere, yet they are fundamental to the issue of revival among the Orthodox. Advocates of revival lean heavily on the female diaconate's supposed apostolic institution and patristic acceptance as sufficient proof that ordaining women as "deacons" or "deaconesses" does not impinge upon any fundamental Christian truth and can therefore be welcomed as fully consistent with Holy Tradition. The evidence will show, if nothing else, that the issue is not nearly that simple. Given ancient Christian understanding of the natural and economic order of the man and the woman, the order of deaconess was inherently problematic for the Church, which explains, with greater ease than anything else, why deaconesses were never universally accepted, why their duties were always very limited, why other duties were not found for them when they were no longer needed to assist in baptism, why the whole Church eventually stopped ordaining them, why the Orthodox Church has gone so long without them, and why the issue of women as deacons is still contested today and cannot be separated from the issue of women as priests, for both issues hinge on the relevance of male and female to the ecclesiastical hierarchy, the social order, and the nature of human being.

CHAPTER 1

Deaconesses Real and Imagined

"The beginnings of a feminine diaconate are indeed hidden in shadow and darkness, and difficult to perceive with any exactness," wrote Roger Gryson in 1972.[1] This no less true today, after nearly half a century of research. The first undisputed evidence of female deacons appears in the third century in the *Didascalia Apostolorum*. Everything before that is a matter of interpretation, and this seems always to have been so. Very early on, the Church developed two traditions concerning the scriptural uses of the words διάκονος, διακονία, and related verbs. Such words appear over a hundred times in the New Testament, and by all accounts only very rarely do they refer in Scripture to the ecclesiastical office of deacon.[2]

Disputed Origins

The basic sense of the verb διακονεῖν is "to serve," "to wait upon," especially "to wait at table." Thus, the servants who filled the jugs with the water turned into wine at the wedding feast of Cana were called διάκονοι (John 2:5–9). But διάκονοι could also mean messengers,

---

[1] Roger Gryson, *The Ministry of Women in the Early Church*, trans. Jean Laporte et al. (Collegeville, Minn.: The Liturgical Press, 1976), originally published as *Le ministère des femmes dans l'Église ancienne* (Gembloux, Belgium: Éditions J. Duculot, 1972), 15.

[2] John Chryssavgis counts 30 uses of διάκονος, 34 uses of διακονία, and 37 uses of related verbs, for a total of 101. See Chryssavgis, *Remembering and Reclaiming Diakonia: The Diaconate Yesterday and Today* (Brookline, Mass.: Holy Cross Orthodox Press, 2009), 24, 31.

representatives, or deputies—someone trusted to do the will of someone greater, a *minister* in the service of a *magister* (whence the English word *master*). Earthly rulers and all Christians are called θεοῦ διάκονοι ("ministers of God") (Rom. 13:4, 2 Cor. 6:4). The Apostle Paul also refers to several specific persons as διάκονοι, including Christ (Rom. 15:8), Apollos (1 Cor. 3:5), Tychicus (Eph. 6:21, Col. 4:7), Epaphras (Col. 1:7), Timothy (1 Thes. 3:2), Paul himself (1 Cor. 3:5; 2 Cor. 3:6, 6:4; Eph. 3:7; Col. 1:23, 25), and Phoebe (Rom. 16:1).

The varied uses of διάκονος make it difficult to say with certainty whether the word indicated a church officer or someone who has provided a service to others. Latin-speaking Christians, having the advantage of two languages, very early adopted the practice of leaving the word διάκονος untranslated but Latinized as *diaconus* when they had reason to believe it meant a church officer, as in the two epistles of Paul that mention διάκονοι in the company of επίσκοποι (Phil. 1:1, 1 Tim. 3). Other uses of διάκονος and διακονία were translated, usually with a form of the verb *ministrare*, whose meaning was nearly identical to διακονεῖν. This translational tradition, distinguishing "deacons" from those who served the Church in less official capacities, persisted in the West long after Westerners became aware of the existence of deaconesses in the East. All early Latin translations of Romans 16:1, including the *Vetus Latina* and St. Jerome's Vulgate, rendered St. Paul's description of Phoebe as *quae est in ministerio,* with one exception: The anonymous fourth-century author known as Ambrosiaster translated the phrase as *quae est ministra.*[3]

Greek-speaking Christians, on the other hand, could not easily distinguish uses of διάκονος as referring to the ecclesiastical office or to the general function of service, and so it is not surprising that some of them later assumed that women associated in Scripture with some form of διακονία were official ministers of the Church. This interpretive tradition is first attested by Clement of Alexandria around AD 200. Commenting on the Apostle Paul's assertion of his right to take along

---

[3] See Aimé Georges Martimort, *Deaconesses: An Historical Study,* trans. K.D. Whitehead (San Francisco: Ignatius Press, 1986), 19. This translational tradition did not begin to change for Western Christians until the latter half of the twentieth century. Eighteen of 54 English-language bibles consulted online at BibleGateway.com identify Phoebe as a "deacon" or "deaconess" in Romans 16:1; all 18 were published after 1950. Just two of the 18 also identify Tychicus and Epaphras as "deacons."

a sister or wife, Clement describes the wives of the Apostles as "fellow-ministers" (συνδιακόνους), saying also that Paul writes Timothy about—in Clement's words—"women deacons" (διακόνων γυναικῶν), presumably a reference to 1 Timothy 3:11, where Paul inserts a mention of women amid his brief discourse on male deacons.[4] A generation later, about the time of the writing of the *Didascalia Apostolorum*, Origen also writes of the early existence of women deacons in his commentary on Romans 16:1, saying, "This text teaches with the authority of the Apostle that even women are instituted deacons in the Church." He goes on to praise Phoebe's hospitality before repeating that the text teaches that "there are, as we have already said, women deacons in the Church."[5]

Doth Origen protest too much? He writes in the present tense, saying there "are" women deacons in the Church, but if there were, would he need to prove it by appealing to Scripture? And is his interpretation of Scripture alone enough to prove the point? Neither he nor Clement gives evidence from their own day to support their interpretation. Neither, for example, mentions deaconesses assisting in baptism or performing any other duty later thought to justify the need for deaconesses. It seems that all they knew of deaconesses was what they read in Scripture, but in arguing from Scripture alone that the Church does have deaconesses, both give evidence that the existence of deaconesses needed argument, which indicates that it was not a fact of life for many Christians in the early third century. That would explain why both Clement and Origen mention deaconesses only exegetically and not when speaking of the Church of their own experience.[6]

In a similar way, St. John Chrysostom gives evidence in the late fourth century that not everyone accepted Clement's reading of 1

---

[4] Clement of Alexandria, *Stromata*, 3.6, PG 8, 1157A–B.

[5] These translations are taken from Gryson, 31. Origen's commentary on Romans survives only in Latin, though the original Greek is not difficult to reconstruct, as Martimort notes. The Latin text, however, avoids the terms "deacon" and "diaconate," writing instead of *feminas in ministerio* and *feminas ministras*. See Martimort, 81–82.

[6] Gryson writes, 32, "Both Clement and Origen occasionally recognized that women were placed in the service of the Church in the time of St. Paul, but they did not indicate that this office survived later, and even less that it existed in Egypt in their own period. When they spoke of the ministries of their era, deaconesses were never mentioned among the ministers of the Church." Martimort concurs, 77–83.

Timothy 3:11.[7] Chrysostom read the verse Clement's way, as a comment on the virtues required of deaconesses, which were known to exist in the East in Chrysostom's time. This is a plausible and perhaps even obvious reading for those who assume, as Chrysostom did, on the basis of Romans 16:1, that deaconesses existed in apostolic times. But the reason Chrysostom gives for his reading is not convincing. He notes that others believe the verse to be about women generally, then asks why Paul would "introduce anything about women to interfere with his subject?"[8] Yet Paul's mention of women interferes with his subject in any case, since his subject before and after verse 11 is *male* deacons.

Were one to read Romans 16:1 in Latin, as later generations of Romans did, without assuming the existence of deaconesses in apostolic times, then a plausible and even obvious reading of 1 Timothy 3:11 would be as a comment on the virtues required of deacons' wives, whom Paul mentions in the next verse: "Let the deacons be the husbands of one wife..."[9] To be sure, St. Paul does not also mention bishops' wives in the preceding verses, but bishops were less likely to have had wives, either because they had followed Paul's example in never marrying or because they were older and widowed. If they were older and still married, their wives could be presumed to have been older and more mature, so Paul would have had less reason to mention them.

We must also ask why Paul was not more inclusive of women when speaking of deacons in 1 Timothy 3. If women were fully deacons in

---

[7] Chrysostom also famously praises Phoebe in his Homily 30 on Romans, saying the Apostle has "added her rank, by mentioning her being [a] 'deaconess.'" (PG 60, 663; NPNF1 11, 549–550) Nevertheless, as Corrado Marucci notes, though Chrysostom mentions Phoebe six times in his many works, he has nothing more to say about her *diakonia*. See Marucci, "The 'Diaconate' of Phoebe (Rom. 16:1–2) According to Modern Exegesis," *Women Deacons: Essays with Answers*, ed. Phyllis Zagano (Collegeville, Minn.: Liturgical Press, 2016), 8–9.

[8] John Chrysostom, Homily 11 on 1 Timothy, PG 62, 553, NPNF1 13, 441.

[9] This is the preferred reading of many scholars, as evidenced by the 54 English-language bibles consulted online at BibleGateway.com, exactly half of which (27) translate γυναῖκας in verse 11 as "wives" instead of "women" to make the meaning of the verse plain. Nevertheless, some scholars believe the verse refers to women generally, for example, J.G. Davies, "Deacons, Deaconesses, and the Minor Orders in the Patristic Period," *The Journal of Ecclesiastical History* 14:1 (April 1963) 1–15.

Paul's time, he would not have needed to make special mention of them, but he begins his discourse speaking only of male deacons, adds a note on women without calling them deacons, then continues as before speaking only of male deacons. Either he is talking about women who are not deacons, or he is talking about women belonging to a separate category of διακονία of lesser concern. Nothing in 1 Timothy makes clear which, and our reading of the passage depends entirely upon our reading of Romans 16:1.

One early pagan text supports the existence of women deacons before the third century: Pliny the Younger's letter to the emperor Trajan, written about 112, in which Pliny reports that he has interrogated two Christian women "who are called ministers" (*quae ministrae dicebantur*).[10] Pliny was governor of the Greek-speaking province of Bithynia and Pontus at the time, so his words could easily be understood as a Latin rendering of what he was told by the women in Greek: They were called διάκονοι by other Christians. Even in Latin, the wording of the letter indicates that the women held a special status in their church, but what that status was is a mystery. The letter doesn't tell us anything more about the women such as what their duties were or what their status as *ministrae* meant to other Christians.[11] Neither does it tell us enough about the women's particular community of Christians for us to guess how well they represented orthodox Christianity. We know from several sources, including some from the second century, that women figured prominently in the leadership of some heretical sects.[12] Pliny may have stumbled upon one of them.

Deacons appear in many early Christian texts without so much as a hint that women were included among them. St. Clement of Rome, St. Ignatius of Antioch, St. Polycarp of Smyrna, St. Justin Martyr, St. Irenaeus of Lyon, the *Didache*, and the *Apostolic Tradition* attributed to St. Hippolytus all mention deacons without explicitly mentioning

---

[10] *Epistolae*, 10.96.8, in S.E. Stout, *Plinius, Epistolae, a Critical Edition*, (Bloomington, Ind.: Indiana University Press, 1962), 355, and Allen Cabaniss, *Pattern in Early Christian Worship* (Macon, Ga.: Mercer University Press, 1989), 91.

[11] Pliny says only, "I deemed it all the more necessary to question under torture two servant girls called *ministrae* and extract from them what was the truth. I discovered nothing, however, but a depraved, extravagant superstition." See Cabaniss, 91.

[12] See Gryson, 15–16.

deaconesses.[13] St. Ignatius and St. Irenaeus also mention specific male deacons. St. Irenaeus tells of a deacon whose wife was led astray, and St. Ignatius commends three deacons by name: "my fellow-servant Burrhus, your deacon," "the deacon Sotio [Zotion], whose friendship may I ever enjoy," and "Philo the deacon, a man of Cilicia."[14]

No Christian text from the Church's first 200 years unambiguously mentions female deacons or deaconesses, generally or specifically, and the first undisputed mention of a deaconess by name does not appear until the fourth century. We are therefore left with three probabilities: Either there were none in the Church's first 200 years, or they were very rare, or they were very rare and became none, disappearing in the first or second century and then reappearing in the third. The order is unquestionably ancient but not unquestionably apostolic, for it remains quite plausible that its appearance in the third century was an innovation inspired by anachronistic readings of Scripture in Greek. Until the late twentieth century, the consensus of modern scholarship favored the Latin way of reading Scripture, doubting that Phoebe was a deacon and understanding 1 Timothy 3:11 to speak of deacons' wives or women generally.[15] Now, however, more scholars read Scripture the Greek way and assume a more egalitarian vision of early Christianity, as we shall see.[16]

---

[13] 1 Clement, 42; St. Ignatius: *Ephesians* 2, 5, *Magnesians* 6, *Trallians* 2, 3, 7, 13, *Philadelphians* 4, 7, 10, 11, *Smyrneans* 8, 9, 12, *Polycarp* 6; St. Polycarp, *Philippians* 5; St. Justin Martyr: *First Apology* 65, 67; St. Irenaeus, *Against Heresies*, 1.13.5; and the *Didache* 15:1.

[14] St. Irenaeus, *Against Heresies*, 1.13.5, PG 7, 588A, ANF 1, 335; St. Ignatius, *Ephesians* 2, PG 5, 645A, ANF 1, 50; *Magnesians* 2, PG 5, 664B, ANF 1, 59; *Philadelphians* 11, PG 5, 705B, ANF 1, 85.

[15] Jean Daniélou accepts that 1 Tim. 3:11 refers to deaconesses but writes of Rom. 16:1, "The word διάκονος, applied to Phoebe, does not really carry with it the sense of a precise ministerial function which it will have later where women are concerned." See Daniélou, *The Ministry of Women in the Early Church*, trans. Glyn Simon (London: The Faith Press, 1961), 7–8. Likewise, Davies, 1–2, writes that there are "no certain references" to women deacons in the New Testament, calling it a "mistake" to assume Phoebe was one. Gryson, 3, and Martimort, 18–20, share this opinion.

[16] On the other hand, Elisabeth Behr-Sigel says the "roots of this feminine ministry unquestionably go back into the apostolic Church although it is difficult to be precise about its nature in the first centuries of the Christian era." Behr-Sigel, *The Ministry of Women in the Church*, Steven Bigham trans. (Redondo Beach, Calif.: Oakwood Publiations, 1991), 171. See also Marucci, 1–12, and Jennifer H. Stiefel, "Women Deacons in 1 Timothy: A Linguistic and

Dubious Sources

Even after deaconesses become a historical reality, they remain a mystery. Nearly all of our detailed information on their duties and status comes from three apocryphal church orders of Syrian origin: the third-century *Didascalia Apostolorum*, the fourth-century *Apostolic Constitutions*, and the fifth-century *Testament of Our Lord Jesus Christ*.[17] All three of these works are believed to have been written originally in Greek, but only the *Constitutions* survives in Greek. None of the three is associated with a local church, and none has received an unqualified stamp of approval from a saint or council of the Orthodox Church.[18] The *Constitutions* was the most widely circulated, but it was rejected by Canon 2 of the Council *in Trullo* in 692 for containing "certain adulterous material . . . clean contrary to piety."[19]

The *Didascalia*, written around 230, gives us our first glimpse of an actual office of deaconess. It is believed to be of Syrian origin in part because of an addition to the analogy made a century earlier by St. Ignatius of Antioch in his epistle to the Magnesians that the faithful are to honor the bishop as God, the deacon as Christ, and the presbyters as the Apostles, to which the *Didascalia* adds the deaconess as the

---

Literary Look at 'Women Likewise ...' (1 Tim. 3:11)," *New Testament Studies* 41 (1995), 13–29.

[17] The *Didascalia Apostolorum* and the *Apostolic Constitutions* claim to be the work of the Apostles; the *Testament of Our Lord* claims Jesus Christ as its author. In contrast, the two earliest church orders, the second-century *Didache* and the early-third-century *Apostolic Tradition* (circa 215), make no claim of authorship—and no mention of deaconesses.

[18] Writing against the Audian heretics of Syria, St. Epiphanius mentions their use of a work that many scholars believe was a form of the *Didascalia*. Epiphanius says this work "is doubted by many but is not discredited. For it contains every canonical regulation and no falsification of the faith" (*Adv. Haer.*, PG 42, 356B–C, *Panarion*, Williams, 412), but he calls this work not the Διδασκαλία of the Apostles but the Διατάξεις of the Apostles, and several of his quotations from the work are not found in the *Didascalia*. Thus, we can hardly say he approved of the *Didascalia* we have today. See James J.C. Cox, *Note on the Title of the* Didascalia Apostolorum, *Andrews University Seminary Studies* (1975), 33.

[19] Canon 2 approves only the 85 Apostolic Canons included in the *Constitutions*, none of which mentions deaconesses. See NPNF2 14, 361. The canons of the Council *in Trullo* are ascribed to the Sixth Ecumenical Council (III Constantinople) in 681 by the Seventh Ecumenical Council (II Nicaea) in 787.

Holy Spirit.[20] In his translator's introduction, R.H. Connolly writes that this is "probably an indication of the oriental associations of the *Didascalia*, since 'spirit' in Semitic languages is feminine."[21] The *Didascalia* does not develop the analogy; it does, however, go to some length to justify the need for deaconesses, another indication that deaconesses were not a well-established tradition in the early third century.[22]

Deacons are mentioned 58 times in Connolly's translation; deaconesses are mentioned just nine times in just two passages, though some mentions of deacons could include women, since the *Didascalia* distinguishes female deacons from male deacons by adding either the word for woman (γύνη διάκονος) or a feminine article (ἡ διάκονος instead of the masculine ὁ διάκονος). The duties of female deacons are summarized in a single passage, worth quoting in full because the concerns expressed about the need for modesty and decency remained the traditional justification for the order of deaconesses as long as it lasted:

> Those that please thee out of all the people thou shalt choose and appoint as deacons: a man for the performance of the most things that are required, but a woman for the ministry of women. For there are houses whither thou canst not send a deacon to the women, on account of the heathen, but mayest send a deaconess. Also, because in many other matters the office of a woman deacon is required. In the first place, when

---

[20] *Didascalia* 9, in R.H. Connolly, *Didascalia Apostolorum* (Oxford: Oxford University Press, 1929), 36. In two other epistles, to the Trallians and to the Smyrneans, St. Ignatius likens the bishop to Christ and deacons to those who serve Christ, but the *Didascalia* follows the form of the analogy in his epistle to the Magnesians. See also Johannes Quasten, *Patrology*, Vol. 2 (Westminster, Md.: Christian Classics, 1983, originally published 1950), 147–152.

[21] Connolly, xlii.

[22] Gryson, 42–43, writes, "Several of these statements [in the *Didascalia*] regarding the ministry of deaconesses sound like pleadings. The author insists on the usefulness, even the necessity, of such a ministry. . . . But it is apparent that there were not deaconesses everywhere, since if no deaconess was present, any woman could serve." Pietro Sorci concurs, characterizing the text as "defensive." See Sorci, "The Diaconate and Other Liturgical Ministries of Women," *Women Deacons: Essays with Answers*, ed. Phyllis Zagano (Collegeville, Minn.: Liturgical Press, 2016), 65.

women go down into the water, those who go down into the water ought to be anointed by a deaconess with the oil of anointing; and where there is no woman at hand, and especially no deaconess, he who baptizes must of necessity anoint her who is being baptized. But where there is a woman, and especially a deaconess, it is not fitting that women should be seen by men. But with the imposition of hand do thou anoint the head only. As of old the priests and kings were anointed in Israel, do thou in like manner, with the imposition of hand, anoint the head of those who receive baptism, whether of men or of women; and afterwards—whether thou thyself baptize, or thou command the deacons or presbyters to baptize—let a woman deacon, as we have already said, anoint the women. But let a man pronounce over them the invocation of the divine Names in the water? And when she who is being baptized has come up from the water, let the deaconess receive her, and teach and instruct her how the seal of baptism ought to be (kept) unbroken in purity and holiness. For this cause we say that the ministry of a woman deacon is especially needful and important. For our Lord and Saviour also was ministered unto by women ministers, *Mary Magdalene, and Mary the daughter of James and mother of Jose, and the mother of the sons of Zebedee* [Matt. 27:56], with other women beside. And thou also hast need of the ministry of a deaconess for many things; for a deaconess is required to go into the houses of the heathen where there are believing women, and to visit those who are sick, and to minister to them in that of which they have need, and to bathe those who have begun to recover from sickness.[23]

The duties of deaconesses are thus to assist in baptism by completing the anointing, to instruct the newly illumined, and to visit women at home among unbelievers, bathing them when sick and assisting those in need, which a man could not do in that world without arousing suspicion or causing scandal.[24]

---

[23] *Didascalia* 16, Connolly, 70–71.
[24] The duties of deacons are similar but much broader and not neatly summarized in the *Didascalia*. Besides tending the sick and needy, they handle

The *Didascalia* says nothing about how women are to be appointed deacons, and the precedents it names (Mary Magdalene, Mary the daughter of James and mother of Joseph, and Mary the mother of James and John) are not identified as "deacons" or "ministers" in Scripture, except in the sense of being said to serve or minister. The duty of instructing newly illumined women is limited by a general prohibition on women teaching, "especially concerning the name of Christ and the redemption of His passion." In support of this limit to women teaching, the *Didascalia* names the same three Marys, saying, "For if it were required that women should teach, our Master Himself would have commanded these to give instruction with us."[25] Likewise, the duty of assisting women in baptism is limited by a general prohibition on women baptizing, in support of which the *Didascalia* says that if Christ had meant women to baptize, he would have been baptized by his mother.[26]

The *Apostolic Constitutions*, written around 380, is a reworking of the *Didascalia* and several other texts.[27] It requires that a deaconess be either a "chaste virgin" (παρθένος ἁγνὴ) or a widow once married.[28] It forbids women to address a deacon or bishop except in the presence of a deaconess, and it forbids deaconesses to act without consulting a deacon.[29] It charges the deaconess with assisting in baptism, minding the women's doors, delivering messages, and distributing aid to needy women, but it omits mention of a catechetical role and clearly distinguishes the offices of deacon and deaconess, saying, "A deaconess does not bless, nor perform anything belonging to the office of presbyters

---

requests and inquiries from the people, question newcomers including women, represent the bishop to the people and the people to the bishop, sit in judgment with the bishop and presbyters, keep order during worship, assist at the altar during the Holy Oblation, and take a vocal role in worship. *Didascalia* 9, 11, 12, 18, Connolly, 38, 48, 54, 56–58, 74, 76.

[25] *Didascalia* 15, Connolly, 63–64.

[26] *Didascalia* 15, Connolly, 67.

[27] The additional material came from the *Didache*, the *Apostolic Tradition*, and the 85 Apostolic Canons. See Quasten, *Patrology*, Vol. 2, 184. The dating of the *Apostolic Constitutions* is based on its mention of Christmas and its doctrine concerning the Holy Spirit, which does not conform to the definition of the Second Ecumenical Council (I Constantinople) in 381. See Paul F. Bradshaw, *The Search for the Origins of Christian Worship* (Oxford: Oxford University Press, second edition 2002), 85.

[28] *Apostolic Constitutions* 6.3.17, ANF 7, 457.

[29] *Apostolic Constitutions* 2.4.26, ANF 7, 410.

or deacons, but only is to keep the doors, and to minister to the presbyters in the baptizing of women, on account of decency."[30]

The status of deaconesses is the *Apostolic Constitutions* is not entirely clear. At times they are mentioned with deacons before subdeacons, readers, and singers; at other times, they are ordered after subdeacons, readers, and singers. Presbyters are ordained in the presence of other presbyters, deacons are ordained in the presence of presbyters and other deacons, and deaconesses are ordained in the presence of presbyters, deacons, and other deaconesses; subdeacons and readers enjoy no such company, and yet the word χειροτονία is used for the ordination of priests, deacons, and subdeacons but not for deaconesses and readers.[31] The prayer for the ordination of a deacon mentions the Protomartyr Stephen, but the prayer for the making of a deaconess mentions only four Old Testament women—the prophetesses Miriam, Deborah, Hannah, and Huldah—perhaps because Phoebe was not universally accepted as a "deacon." (As we shall see later, Western Christians still resisted this reading of Romans 16:1.)

The deaconess is likened to the Holy Spirit in the *Apostolic Constitutions*, as in the *Didascalia*, but she is also plainly subordinated to the deacon: "Let also the deaconess be honoured by you in the place of the Holy Ghost, and not do or say anything without the deacon; as neither does the Comforter say or do anything of Himself, but gives glory to Christ by waiting for His pleasure."[32] The *Apostolic Constitutions* empowers a deacon to "separate" subdeacons, readers, chanters, or deaconesses when a presbyter is not present, but it expressly forbids subdeacons, readers, chanters, and deaconesses to separate anyone, "for they are the ministers to the deacons."[33] It specifies the order at Communion as bishop, presbyters, deacons, subdeacons, readers, chanters, monks, and then deaconesses, followed by virgins, widows, children, and the rest of the people.[34] Of the leftover offerings, it allots four portions to the bishop, three to the priests, two to the deacons,

---

[30] *Apostolic Constitutions* 3.2, ANF 7, 431; 3.2.19, ANF 7, 432; 3.1.14, ANF 7, 430; 8.3.28, ANF 7, 494.

[31] *Apostolic Constitutions* 8.3.16–22, ANF 7, 492.

[32] *Apostolic Constitutions* 2.4.26, ANF 7, 410.

[33] *Apostolic Constitutions* 8.3.28, ANF 7, 494.

[34] *Apostolic Constitutions* 8.3.13, ANF 7, 490.

and one to the subdeacons, readers, chanters, and deaconesses, again in that order.[35]

The status of deaconesses is even less clear in the fifth-century *Testament of Our Lord Jesus Christ*, which favors widows over deaconesses in a way seen nowhere else. The *Testament* provides a prayer for the making of widows but not for the making of deaconesses. It honors widows as "those who sit up front" but stations deaconesses at the door of the church.[36] During the Oblation, the *Testament* positions widows behind presbyters on the left, with deacons behind presbyters on the right, readers behind deacons, subdeacons behind readers, and deaconesses behind subdeacons.[37] It assigns widows the tasks of anointing women after baptism, visiting women in their homes, instructing women, and even vetting women to be deaconesses.[38] Other than minding the door, the only duty assigned to deaconesses is taking Communion to pregnant women unable to be in church on Pascha.[39] The order at Communion is: bishops, presbyters, deacons, widows, readers, subdeacons, and "finally those with special charisms and the newly baptized and the boys. The people, however, [receive] in this order: elderly men, celibates, then the rest. From among the women: first the deaconesses, then the others."[40]

The *Testament of Our Lord* follows the third-century *Apostolic Tradition* attributed to St. Hippolytus of Rome in allowing widows

---

[35] *Apostolic Constitutions* 8.4.31, ANF 7, 494.

[36] *Testament of Our Lord*, 1.19.

[37] *Testament of Our Lord*, 1.23.

[38] *Testament of Our Lord*, 2.20, 2.8, and 1.40: "Let her instruct those women who do not obey; let her teach those [women] who have not learnt; let her convert those who are foolish; let her instruct them to be grave; let her prove the deaconesses; let her make those who enter to know of what sort and who they are; also let her instruct them that they abide." English translation from Syriac by J. Cooper and A.J. Maclean, *The Testament of Our Lord* (Edinburgh, 1902), 106.

[39] *Testament of Our Lord*, 1.19; 2.20.

[40] *Testament of Our Lord*, 1.23. This translation, with the insertion, is Robert Taft's. The "boys" refer either to young acolytes or to the "little singing-boys" mentioned in the *Testament*'s book 2, chapters 11, 22, and 26. See Robert F. Taft, "Women at Church in Byzantium: Where, When—and Why?" *Dumbarton Oaks Papers*, 52 (1998), 81–82. Other translations say "babes" instead of "boys," consistent with the order of communion in the *Apostolic Constitutions*, which puts children before adults. See *Apostolic Constitutions* 8.3.13, ANF 7, 490.

pride of place over minor clergy, but who are its deaconesses? The *Apostolic Tradition* doesn't mention deaconesses, and the *Testament of Our Lord* doesn't clearly define them. Are they a subset of widows or a separate order? The image is so uncertain that Evangelos Theodorou conflates the two, writing of "widow-deaconesses" and "deacon-widows."[41] Yet the author of the *Testament* plays down deaconesses, limiting their duties, exalting widows over them, and even charging the deacon with calling out their names when they arrive late, that people might pray for them.[42] Aimé Georges Martimort suggests a possible explanation: The author only knows deaconesses from his source documents and is therefore reluctant to make too much of them.[43] But another possible explanation is that the *Testament* bears witness to reaction against deaconesses, which will show up later in Syrian writers and may also be seen in the "ambivalence" Paul Bradshaw sees in the East Syrian rite of ordination of deaconesses.[44]

Historical Record

Deaconesses appear with greater historical certainty in Canon 19 of the First Ecumenical Council (I Nicaea) in 325. Here for the first time we have an undisputed reference to actual deaconesses, not just the hypothetical deaconesses of apocryphal church orders.[45] And here also for the first time the gender-specific neologism διακόνισσα (whence "deaconess") is used, but it is used in reference to the

---

[41] Evangelos Theodorou, "The Institution of Deaconesses in the Orthodox Church and the Possibility of Its Restoration," The Place of the Woman in the Orthodox Church and the Question of the Ordination of Women: InterOrthodox Symposium, Rhodos, Greece, 30 October–7 November 1988, ed. Gennadios Limouris (Katerini, Greece: Tertios Publications, 1992), 219.

[42] *Testament of Our Lord*, 1.36.

[43] Martimort, 50.

[44] Paul Bradshaw notes that the East Syrian rite for ordaining a deaconess does not immediately follow the rite for ordaining deacons and "tends to be described as a blessing rather than an ordination." The rite is performed in the sacristy instead of the church, and it omits several features in the Byzantine rite such as vesting with an orarion that make the ordination seem more diaconal. See Paul F. Bradshaw, *Ordination Rites of the Ancient Churches of East and West* (New York: Pueblo Publishing Company, 1990), 90–91.

[45] The Orthodox Church honors the Venerable Platonida of Nisibis in Syria (+308) as an abbess and deaconess, but our knowledge of her is solely hagiographic, and it is impossible to know whether the identification of her as a deaconess is not a later tradition.

deaconesses of the Paulianist sect, followers of the heretic and repro-
bate Paul of Samosata (modern Samsat in southeast Turkey).[46] The issue is how such deaconesses are to be readmitted to the Church, and
the decision of the council is that they are to be received as laity, since
they have received "no imposition of hands" (χειροθεσία).[47]

Canon 19 has been variously interpreted. Some see it as evidence
that, unlike Paulianist deaconesses, orthodox deaconesses received an
imposition of hands and were therefore ranked among the clergy
(κλῆρος); others argue the opposite—that an imposition of hands was
also not usual for orthodox deaconesses, so they were not ranked
among the clergy.[48] Neither of these possibilities can be excluded
without knowing or assuming more about the existence of deaconesses
among the orthodox in the early fourth century.[49] All that can be said

---

[46] Paul of Samosata was condemned and deposed for monarchianism and corruption in 269.

[47] Canon 19 states in full: "Concerning the Paulianists who have flown for ref-
uge to the Catholic Church, it has been decreed that they must by all means be
rebaptized; and if any of them who in past time have been numbered among
their clergy should be found blameless and without reproach, let them be rebaptized and ordained by the Bishop of the Catholic Church; but if the examination should discover them to be unfit, they ought to be deposed. Likewise
in the case of their deaconesses, and generally in the case of those who have
been enrolled among their clergy, let the same form be observed. And we mean
by deaconesses such as have assumed the habit, but who, since they have no
imposition of hands, are to be numbered only among the laity." NPNF₂ 14, 40.

[48] The former argument is made by Valerie A. Karras, "Female Deacons in the
Byzantine Church," *Church History*, 73:2 (June 2004), 287–290; the latter
argument is made by Adolf Kalsbach, Gryson, 48–49, and Martimort, 101–
104, with Martimort suggesting the bishops at Nicaea were unfamiliar with
deaconesses. Likewise, Sorci, 72, writes, "From the text it seems that the council is not aware of a rite of ordination for deaconesses." On the other hand,
Cipriano Vagaggini, after much argumentation against Kalsbach and Gryson,
concludes that Canon 19 could be understood either way and perhaps was understood both ways in the fourth century. See Vagaggini, "The Ordination of
Deaconesses in the Greek and Byzantine Tradition," *Women Deacons: Essays
with Answers*, ed. Phyllis Zagano (Collegeville, Minn.: Liturgical Press, 2016),
114.

[49] As it happens, Eusebius of Caesarea preserves large portions of the synodal
letter issued by the Council of Antioch in 265 condemning Paul of Samosata.
The letter mentions Paul's presbyters and deacons and his "spiritual brides, as
the Antioch people call them." It also condemns Paul for resisting the singing
of traditional hymns to Christ at Pascha and having a choir of women sing
praises to himself instead. Are these "spiritual brides" or the women's choir
Paul's deaconesses? Neither the synod nor Eusebius mentions deaconesses,

for certain is that an imposition of hands was usual for members of the orthodox clergy, and therefore Paulianist deaconesses were not clergy.

There can be no doubt, however, that before the end of the fourth century deaconesses did exist among the orthodox, did receive an imposition of hands, were sometimes counted as clergy, and were sometimes *not* counted as clergy, just like today's subdeacons and readers. Before his death in 379, St. Basil the Great wrote to his fellow bishop Amphilochius three long epistles reporting the results of his inquiry into customary rules of church discipline. Canon 3 says that a deacon guilty of fornication should receive the clerical penalty of permanent deposition without excommunication, whereas Canon 44 says that a deaconess guilty of fornication should receive the lay penalty of temporary excommunication. In explaining the deacon's penalty, Basil appeals to an old rule, in Apostolic Canon 25, "Thou shalt not avenge twice for the same thing"—a clear indication that the Church of St. Basil's day did not consider deacons and deaconesses to be ordinationally equal.[50]

Writing about the same time, St. Epiphanius of Salamis divided the clergy into two groups: the priesthood (ἱερωσύνη), consisting of bishops, presbyters, deacons, and subdeacons, and those ordered "after the priesthood," including readers, deaconesses, exorcists, interpreters, undertakers, doorkeepers.[51] Discoursing against the Collyridians, who worshipped the Virgin Mary, he writes:

> It is plain too that there is an order of deaconesses in the church. But this is not allowed for the practice of priesthood or any liturgical function, but for the sake of female modesty, at either the time of baptism or of the examination of some condition or trouble, and when a woman's body may be bared,

---

but this could be because neither the synod nor Eusebius approved of deaconesses or knew much about them. *Ecclesiastical History*, 7.30, PG 20 709–720.
[50] The deacon's penalty is found in Letter 188, Canon 3, PG 32, 672BC; the deaconess's in Letter 199, Canon 44, PG 32, 729B. Apostolic Canon 25, which prohibits punishing someone twice for the same offense, is based on Nahum 1:9.
[51] *Adversus Haereses: Expositio Fidei*, PG 42, 824, in *The Panarion of Epiphanius of Salamis*, Vol. 2, trans. Frank Williams (New York: E.J. Brill, 1994), 662. See also Vagaggini, "The Ordination of Deaconesses in the Greek and Byzantine Tradition," 116–117.

so that she will not be seen by the male priests but by the assisting female who is appointed by the priest for the occasion, to take care of the woman who is in need of it when her body is uncovered.[52]

Here St. Epiphanius plainly accepts the existence of deaconesses in the Church but gives no indication of any actual experience with deaconesses, which leaves open the possibility that he is only repeating what he has heard from others or read in the *Didascalia* or *Apostolic Constitutions*.[53]

Deaconesses are first mentioned by name in the literature of the late fourth century. Few of these mentions tell us much about deaconesses, but some deaconesses are said to head groups of virgins. There is Lampadia, who is said by St. Gregory of Nyssa to have headed a group of virgins present at the funeral of his sister, St. Macrina. There is also Marthana, who is said by the pilgrim Egeria to have ruled over ascetics of the Apotactic heresy in Palestine.

Then there is Chrysostom's friend and ally St. Olympias, the deaconess about whom we know the most. The aristocratic Olympias was widowed at an early age before becoming a mother. The emperor St. Theodosius the Great wanted her to remarry a member of his court, but she refused, so he sequestered her sizable fortune until she reached the age of 30, upon which she began funding charitable works benefiting the Church, founding a hospital, a hospice for priests, and a monastery for women. In gratitude, the archbishop St. Nectarius made her a deaconess in 390. That same year, the emperor Theodosius issued a decree setting the minimum age for deaconesses at 60, the age the Apostle Paul set for enrolled widows in 1 Timothy 5:9, which the legislation mentions.[54] The fifth-century church historian Sozomen vaguely relates this legislation to sexual scandal, but Olympias's

---

[52] *Adv. Haer.*, PG 42, 745, in *Panarion*, trans. Williams, Vol. 2, 623.
[53] See Martimort, 114.
[54] The required age for deaconesses changed several times over the years: Canon 15 of Chalcedon in 451 lowered it to 40; Justinian's Novella 6 in 535 raised it to 50; Justinian's Novella 123 in 546 lowered it to 40 again; and Canon 14 of the Council *in Trullo* in 692 confirmed it at 40.

early elevation to the dignity of deaconess might have had more to do with it.[55]

The conflict of interests in Olympias's case is obvious: The state's interest was seeing rich young widows married to strengthen political alliances, commit their wealth to public use, and keep down expenses for state-supported clergy; the Church's interest was encouraging the piety and patronage of wealthy women, and making them deaconesses was one of the few means of doing that. It should not surprise us, then, that deaconesses thereafter became a fixture in the imperial capital as well as the subject of further regulation by other emperors such as St. Justinian, who in 535 set the required age for deaconesses at 50 and limited their number supported by the Great Church in Constantinople to 40, compared to 60 priests, 100 deacons, 90 subdeacons, 110 readers, and 25 chanters.[56]

As in the *Apostolic Constitutions* and *Testament of Our Lord*, the status of Justinian's deaconesses *vis-à-vis* other clergy is not entirely clear in imperial legislation. They are sometimes included in a mention of clergy and sometimes added to a mention of clergy, as in Justinian's mention of "a cleric, a monk, a deaconess, a nun, or an ascetic."[57] They are often paired with deacons and in such cases are named before subdeacons and readers, but this may be merely a stylistic convenience on account of the similarity of names for the offices of deacon and deaconess, in no way indicative of their ranking among the clergy or order at Communion, as we have seen in the *Apostolic Constitutions*. They are sometimes called "female deacons" and sometimes called "deaconesses," but deacons' wives were also called "deaconesses," which may explain the use of "female deacons."

---

[55] Sozomen first tells a story that also appears in the history of his contemporary Socrates about a laywoman raped by a deacon, then says merely, "I believe it was from similar considerations" that Theodosius enacted his law concerning deaconesses. A more plausible explanation involving Olympias is made by Susanna Elm, *Virgins of God: The Making of Asceticism in Late Antiquity* (Oxford: Clarendon Press, 1994), 178–183. For Sozomen's account, see his *Ecclesiastical History* 7.16, PG 67, 1457–1464, NPNF2 2, 387. For Socrates's account, see his *Ecclesiastical History* 5.19, PG 67, 613–620, NPNF2 2, 128. Socrates does not connect the rape to the legislation.

[56] *Novellae* 3 and 6, dated March 16, 535. Novella 6 makes an exception to the minimum age of 50 for younger women living in hermitages and having no contact with men.

[57] *Novella* 3 of 535 and *Novella* 123 of 546, in Martimort, 110–111.

It is nevertheless clear in the *novellae* of Justinian that deaconesses do not have the same standing as male deacons. Their minimum age is twice that of deacons. They must be widows, virgins, or wives separated from their husbands on account of their husbands becoming bishops or monks. Penalties for misbehavior are much more severe. In *Novella* 6 of 535, Justinian likens deaconesses to the Vestal Virgins of pagan Rome and decrees for them the same punishment for forsaking their vow of chastity—death, although this was likely a symbolic penalty never actually imposed. In *Novella* 123 of 546, Justinian reduced the penalty for deaconesses to confinement to a monastery and forfeiture of all property, in contrast to deposition and forfeiture of all property for deacons.[58]

It is in making his case for capital punishment in 535 that Justinian mentions the deaconess's "priesthood" (ἱερωσύνη) and "sacred ordination" (ἱερὰ χειροτονία).[59] Much has been made lately of the difference in usage of the words χειροτονία and χειροθεσία. The Byzantines did sometimes reserve χειροτονία for higher orders, but Canon 15 of the Fourth Ecumenical Council (Chalcedon, 451) uses both words in setting the minimum age for deaconesses at 40, and Canons 2 and 6 of Chalcedon use χειροτονία for lower orders as well, as did later Byzantines such as the canonist Matthew Blastares, who wrote in the fourteenth century of the χειροτονία of readers.[60] Even when higher and lower forms of ordination were distinguished, the line was not always drawn between the same ranks. Canon 10 of Antioch in 341 uses the word καθίστημι for subdeacons and readers and χειροτονία for priests and deacons, but Canon 6 of the Council *in Trullo* in 692 uses χειροτονία for priests, deacons, and subdeacons.[61] Our modern manner of distinguishing "major clergy" and "minor clergy" is itself not consistent with our χειροτονία of subdeacons. We can hardly expect

---

[58] Karras (2004), 294–296, attributes these "double standards" to "cultural notions" and "cultural bias."

[59] *Novella* 6, in Martimort, 110–111.

[60] *Syntagma, littera Chi*, PG 145, 200. For other uses, see Martimort, 147, n. 8.

[61] Canon 10 of Antioch concerns the powers of *chorepiscopi* ("country bishops"), who are allowed to appoint subdeacons and readers but not ordain priests and deacons. Canon 6 of *Trullo* concerns who among clerics may marry: Readers may because they have not been "ordained"; subdeacons, deacons, and priests may not because they have been "ordained."

greater consistency from the Byzantines, of whom Robert F. Taft says, "nothing was more foreign to the Byzantines than terminological precision."[62]

But what did Justinian's deaconesses do?

The duties of clergy were not often the subject of imperial legislation, but Justinian in 535 does mention one specific duty of deaconesses—assisting at baptism, which by then could not have been very demanding after two centuries of Christian rule. The Church still baptized the occasional convert from heresy, paganism, or Judaism, but infant baptism had all but dried up the catechumenate.[63]

The legislation also speaks of "other hidden tasks that they normally carry out in connection with the most venerable mysteries," but this is either a polite catchall for duties too minor to mention or a face-saving phrase for an office that was then essentially honorary and without important purpose.[64] Contemporaneous support for the latter is provided by Severus of Antioch in a letter written sometime between 518 and 538 in response to a query about how anti-Chalcedonian churches are to ordain clergy while under Chalcedonian persecution. He answers, "In the case of deaconesses, especially in convents, ordination is performed less with regard to the needs of the mysteries than exclusively with regards to doing honor."[65]

Monasticism and Ordination

For several centuries, the duty most in evidence for deaconesses was management of female monastics. The relationship of deaconesses to widows and virgins is not easy to trace, but in time the orders

---

[62] Taft, 54. In the same work, 31, he writes of the "maddening insouciance with which the Byzantines threw around terms." His comments are prompted by the variability in architectural terminology, which makes it difficult to tell what part of a church a text is talking about, but his words ring equally true for many other terms.

[63] Taft, 60–62, cites St. Maximus the Confessor's commentary on the *Ecclesiastical Hierarchy* of Pseudo-Dionysius as indicating that, within a century of Justinian's legislation, the actual dismissal of the catechumens from the Divine Liturgy had become a dead letter—something said but not done.

[64] *Novella* No. 6, dated March 16, 535, quoted in Martimort, 112. Taft, 34, says the duty of keeping order in the *gynaeceum* in church is attested in Constantinople as early as the time of St. Gregory the Theologian, but this was hardly a "hidden task."

[65] Martimort, 128.

of widows, virgins, and deaconesses coalesced into communities of nuns, with deaconesses often taking the lead. Wealthy, educated, aristocratic women were well suited for this task. Some who were made deaconesses had already founded their own monastic houses. Susanna Elm suggests that making deaconesses of such women may have been a means not only of rewarding their piety and benevolence but also of co-opting potential troublemakers by bringing them under clerical control and busying them with monastic duties:

> In all of these endeavors, the main challenge facing the clergy was to gain and preserve the support of female ascetics—often the possessors of vast financial resources and high-ranking connections, as exemplified by Olympias—without granting these women any degree of public influence that could threaten its own prerogatives.[66]

The rank of deaconess and the office of abbess did not always go hand in hand, however. There were abbesses who were not deaconesses, and deaconesses who were not abbesses.[67] But before the Church adopted a standard blessing for abbesses, the ordination of deaconesses sometimes served that purpose. Three Syrian texts connect ordination as a deaconess with the office of abbess. The first was written between 532 and 534 and consists of responses from Jacobite bishops in exile in Antioch to questions asked by Jacobite priests farther east, perhaps in Persia. Its Canon 9 says:

> The custom of the East, namely, that the superiors of female monasteries should be deaconesses and should share the mysteries with those who are under their power, should be preserved everywhere there is a deaconess, if there is no priest or deacon in the place where the mysteries are shared; but if

---

[66] See Elm, 182–183.

[67] When Olympias went into exile, she left her monastery in the hands of Marina, who is not said to have been a deaconess, but when Marina died she was succeeded by Elisanthia, who *is* said to have already been a deaconess. See Martimort, 135–137.

there is in the vicinity a pure priest or a deacon, then the superiors should not give out [Communion].[68]

Canon 10 then directs that the ordination of deaconesses should follow local custom, noting that "we have also learned that the bishop casts an orarion on the shoulder of the candidate, as is the case for the deacon."[69]

The second text, dated 538, contains responses from John bar Qursos, bishop of Tella, near Edessa, to questions from a priest named Sargis. It specifies the cans and can'ts of the office of deaconess. The latter text reveals two obvious concerns: providing for the needs of female monastic communities and preserving the male character of the priesthood. The deaconess may therefore enter the altar to assist the priest when there is no deacon present, fill the chalice with wine and water before the Holy Oblation, read the Gospels and other Scriptures in assemblies of women, commune children under five years of age, wash the utensils used in the Holy Oblation, and authorize another woman to enter the altar to wash the utensils and dispose of candles when she herself is too sick to do so. She may not, however, enter any altar other than her own, enter her own altar when a deacon is present, enter the altar or touch the Holy Gifts when menstruating, bless the censer, raise her voice in church while censing, or commune children five years old or older.[70]

The third and much later text from Syria is the *Canonical Resolutions* of James of Edessa, written around 700. It permits deaconesses to anoint women after baptism, to care for sick women, and when no priest or deacon is present, to sweep the altar, light candles in the altar, and remove the Holy Gifts from the wall cabinet in which they were kept and give them to women and small children. They may not, however, place the Holy Gifts on the altar table, remove the Holy Gifts from the altar table, or touch the altar table for any reason.[71]

The age limitation, in two of these texts, for both boys and girls to whom a deaconess may administer Holy Communion is especially

---

[68] In Martimort, 140, citing I. Rahmani, *Studia syrica* 3.
[69] Martimort, 140.
[70] See Martimort, 140–142, citing A. Vööbus, *Syrische Kanonessammlungen*, CSCO 317, 263–269.
[71] Martimort, 142–143.

telling. Part of growing up is learning the difference between men and women. These bishops of the East presumably feared that older boys and girls receiving Communion from deaconesses might grow up to see women as priests or deacons. To guard against this, they allowed deaconesses to commune only very young children and grown women, a practice that would have not only avoided creating the wrong impression in children but also provided an occasion for teaching children proper respect for divinely ordained gender differences.[72]

With this image in mind, of an abbess in monastery serving only women and children, without the aid of a deacon or any other male cleric, without even the presence of a priest at times, we are now ready to examine the rite of ordination of deaconesses preserved in a handful of Byzantine euchologies dating from the eighth to the fourteenth century, for only in a monastery do we see deaconesses doing anything remotely resembling the work of deacons in church.[73]

The first obvious fact about these rites is that they occur not in the midst of the church before the Divine Liturgy, as ordinations of subdeacons and readers do, but at the altar after the consecration of the Holy Gifts, just when deacons are ordained. If in the fourth century deaconesses ranked after subdeacons, readers, and even chanters, in these euchologies they appear to rank above those three.[74]

The second obvious fact about these rites is that the ordination of a deaconess is not simply the ordination of a deacon and that the two ordinations are not "virtually identical," as some have claimed.[75] The

---

[72] Today the churching of male and female newborns differently provides a similar opportunity for teaching respect for gender differences, although the opportunity is often ignored and the difference in churching is sometimes eliminated because the Church's teaching on the subject is no longer believed by many people, in some cases because they have never heard it.

[73] The high-end estimate of Byzantine euchologies is 2,000; less than a dozen are known to contain rites for ordaining deaconesses. Theodorou names six, and Martimort names nine, for a total of ten named euchologies between them. The oldest is the Barberini Codex Gr. 336 in the Vatican Library. There is little difference in the rites among the ten. Most of the differences are additions to the rubrics of the later euchologies. See Martimort, 149–151, and Theodorou, "Service of God and Service of Man," *Theologia*, 68:3 (July-September 1997), 425.

[74] See Vagaggini, "The Ordination of Deaconesses in the Greek and Byzantine Tradition," 135–139.

[75] The claim that the two rites are "virtually identical" is made by Karras (2004), 275, and repeated in Karras "The Liturgical Function of Consecrated

26

form is the same, but the content of the form is differentiated at every opportunity. A deaconess does not kneel or rest her head on the Holy Table, as deacons and priests do; she merely bows her head.[76] The bishop says two prayers over her, as he does for deacons, but there is, as Valerie Karras admits, "almost no textual correspondence" between them.[77] Paul Bradshaw notes that the prayers for ordaining a deaconess express the woman's desire to serve and voluntary offering of herself, whereas the prayers for ordaining a deacon declare God's will in having selected and appointed a man to serve, suggesting that deacons were viewed as essential to the Church but deaconesses were not.[78] A deaconess is not given a fan (*rapidion*) to hold over the Holy Gifts, as deacons are. She does receive a stole (*orarion*), but it is placed not over her left shoulder, as for deacons, but around her neck so that both ends hang down in front—under her *maphorion*, the hooded mantle commonly worn by women, as in every icon of the Theotokos. Her head would thus have been covered during her ordination, unlike a deacon's. At Communion, she is not given a chalice to carry out to the people, as deacons are; instead, after partaking of the Chalice, she takes it from the bishop and immediately returns it to the Holy Table. Finally, she does not intone the Litany of Thanksgiving after Communion, as a newly ordained deacon does.[79]

The third obvious fact about the ordination rites is that there is little in them suggesting the duties most often associated with deaconesses—assisting at baptism, visiting women at home, or carrying Communion to women not in church. Neither is there anything to suggest service in the altar beyond the act of returning the Chalice to the Holy Table. The prayers said over a deaconess do not speak of a ministry

---

Women in the Byzantine Church," *Theological Studies*, 66 (2005), 96. Theodorou (1992), 213, makes a similar claim that the rites are "absolutely uniform."

[76] Pseudo-Dionysius writes that only those ordained to leadership roles kneel during ordination, noting that monks do not kneel when they are tonsured as monks but saying nothing of deaconesses. See Pseudo-Dionysius, *Ecclesiastical Hierarchy* 6.3.1, PG 3, 533C, and John Ramsey, *The Minor Clergy of the Orthodox Church: Their Role and Life according to the Canons* (John Ramsey, 2016), 56.

[77] See Karras (2004), 302.

[78] See Bradshaw (1990), 88–89.

[79] For more analysis, see Bradshaw (1990), 88–89, 136–139; Theodorou (1992), 207–238; Martimort, 148–156; and Karras (2004), 296–309.

related to "immaculate mysteries," as the prayers said over deacons and subdeacons do. Instead, the second ordination prayer for a deaconess speaks of ministering "in your holy houses" (τοῖς ἁγίος οἴκοις) and of diligence in "domestic conduct" (τῆς οἰκείας πολιτείας).[80] Neither of these phrases appears in the prayers said over deacons or subdeacons. They may refer to the duty of keeping order in the *gynaeceum*, but they more likely to refer to life in a convent. Only in convents do we see deaconesses providing limited assistance in the altar, including cleaning up and (we might say) putting away the dishes, which the act of returning the Chalice may symbolize. The rite therefore seems to have been written for a nun in a nunnery. It is essentially a monastic rite.

But it was not written necessarily for the ordination of abbesses, for there is also Canon 48 of the Council *in Trullo*, which requires the wives of men elevated to the episcopate to separate from their husbands and enter a monastery, "and if she is deemed worthy she may be advanced to the dignity of a deaconess."[81] These words could mean merely that bishops' wives are not barred from becoming deaconesses on account of being still married, but they seem to hold out the honor of becoming a deaconess as an incentive for wives to consent to their husbands becoming bishops.[82] This strengthens the connection of deaconesses to monasteries, but it also weakens the connection of deaconesses to both the office of abbess and the needs of the altar, giving us another reason to believe Severus of Antioch when he says that "especially in convents" the order was largely honorary. If it was, the surviving ordination rite may not reflect the actual status, dress, or duties of a deaconess. Donning an orar and returning the Chalice to the Holy Table could have been purely symbolic acts, flattering to the ordinand

---

[80] Martimort, 150, translates τῆς οἰκείας πολιτείας as "household governance," which Bradshaw (1990), 271, says seems "improbably narrow." Bradshaw translates the phrase as "appropriate conduct," but that seems just as improbably broad. Appropriate for what?

[81] NPNF2 14, 388.

[82] Karras writes: "By the middle Byzantine period, bishops typically took monastic vows, so the monastic tonsure combined with ordination to the female diaconate was as near as the wife of a bishop could get to her (former) husband's ecclesiastical 'rank.' There is no indication, however, that bishops' wives-cum-deaconesses were expected to have any particular liturgical or other ministry. Presumably they served the same functions as other deaconesses within a monastery setting." See Karras (2004), 282.

but not intended to be repeated after ordination, like the present practice of placing a shortened *phelonion* on the shoulders of a reader at
his tonsuring to symbolize that he has taken the first step toward the
priesthood.[83]

Distribution and Disappearance

By now, it should be obvious that the place of deaconesses in the
early Church was greatly limited, not just liturgically but also geo-
graphically. Nearly all of our information about them comes from
Syria or Constantinople. They appear in inscriptions most often in
Asia Minor, the land between Syria and Constantinople.[84] They were
certainly present elsewhere, but not everywhere, and not anywhere
else in such numbers that much was said about them. This is not what
we would expect from a tradition of the first century begun by the
Apostles themselves; it is what we would expect from a Syrian innovation of the third century not entirely consistent with apostolic tradition.

Deaconesses do not appear in the West for several centuries. They
are not mentioned in St. Hippolytus of Rome's *Apostolic Tradition* or
in the letter written around 300 by Pope Cornelius of Rome to the patriarch of Antioch providing staffing numbers for the Church in
Rome.[85] They are also not mentioned by the great Latin-language
writers of Africa: Tertullian, St. Cyprian of Carthage, and St. Augustine
of Hippo. The first word we hear in Latin of deaconesses is a fourth-
century condemnation by Ambrosiaster, who dismissed them as a
"foolish presumption" (*vana praesumptione*) of the Cataphrygians
(Montanists).[86]

Several early Gallic councils banned deaconesses, beginning with
the anti-Priscillianist Council of Nîmes in 396, which speaks of women

---

[83] Karras notes the "complete lack of visual evidence" of deaconesses wearing
orars, in contrast to the traditional depiction of Sts. Stephen and Lawrence.
See Karras (2004), 307.
[84] Karras (2004), 274, notes "ample literary evidence of a female diaconate in
the capital city, and archeological evidence of deaconesses in a number of
other areas of the Empire, particularly Asia Minor."
[85] The count included 46 priests, 7 deacons, 7 subdeacons, 42 acolytes, and 52
exorcists, readers, and janitors, plus over 1,500 widows on the rolls. Martimort, 187–188.
[86] *Commentary on 1 Timothy*, PL 17, 70C, in Martimort, 191.

deacons as "unseemly" (*indecens*) and "irregular" (*contra rationem facta*), "a thing unheard of until now" (*incognito usque in hoc tempus*) and even now only heard of somewhere unknown (*nescio quo loco*).[87] Afterwards came condemnations by the councils of Orange in 441, Epaone in 517, and Orleans in 533.[88] Martimort reasons that some bishops resorted to blessing widows as deaconesses because the West then had no other way of making nuns of women who were not virgins, but that their brother bishops did not approve.[89] Two canons of the Second Council of Orleans in 533 suggest a reason: Canon 17 excommunicates deaconesses who remarry, and Canon 18 directs that such blessings cease on account of "the frailty of her sex."[90] It seems that too many deaconesses were not living up to their honor. There is also an early sixth-century letter from three Gallic bishops condemning the "novelty" of women distributing communion, which is blamed on "Pepodian" heretics, presumably Montanists.[91]

Deaconesses are known in Italy from the seventh century, when parts of Italy were still under Byzantine rule, but they are not attested in Rome until around 799, when they were among the people who

---

[87] The acts of the council do not use the words *diacona* or *diaconissa* but refer instead to a "levitical" ministry of women, a common way to speak of diaconal ministry. See Martimort, 193.

[88] Orange: "In no way whatsoever should deaconesses ever be ordained. If there already are, they should bow their heads beneath the blessing which is given to all the people" (Martimort, 193). Epaone: "We completely suppress throughout our territory the consecration of those widows who are often called 'deaconesses'; if they wish to convert, only penitential benediction may be conferred on them" (Gryson, 107).

[89] The consecration of virgins was accomplished by an elaborate veiling ceremony (*velatio virginis*) resembling a wedding. There was nothing similar for widows or wives wanting to live as nuns. We know of at least one married woman in Gaul, the Frankish queen St. Radegunde of Poitiers, who begged a bishop to make her a deaconess in the sixth century. After that time, a blessing for widows was added to the service books, and the prohibition on the "veiling" of non-virgins was a relaxed. See Martimort, 198–200.

[90] Canon 17: "Foeminae, quae benedictionem diaconatus hactenus contra interdicta canonum acceperunt, si ad coniugium probantur iterum devolutae, a communione pellantur. Quod si huiusmodi contubernium admonitae ab espiscopo cognito errore dissolverint, in communionis gratia acta paenitentia reuertantur" (Martimort, 197–198). Canon 18: "Placuit etiam, ut nulli postmodum feminae diaconalis benediction pro conditionis huius fragilitate credatur" (Martimort, 199). See also Gryson, 107.

[91] Martimort, 195.

went out to greet Pope Leo III at the Milvian Bridge.[92] Who these deaconesses were and what they did are mysteries. The mystery is com-
plicated by the custom of calling clergy wives by the feminine form of
their husband's rank: *episcopissa, presbyterissa, diaconissa*. But
there is evidence of *diaconissae* in Italy who were not deacons' wives,
as well as evidence that *diaconissa* was often understood in the West
to mean *abbatissa*.[93] This was perhaps how a ninth-century bishop of
Calabria understood *diaconissa* when he wrote to Patriarch Photius of
Constantinople asking who should carry Holy Communion to Christians held by the Saracens; Photius advised him to make a few "noble
women" deaconesses, an answer the Calabrian bishop would not have
needed had customs in Calabria matched customs in Constantinople.[94]

The West was not the only region not to follow the customs of Constantinople. Evidence of deaconesses in Egypt is so scant that many
scholars have assumed the Egyptians did not ordain them.[95] Ugo Zanetti argues persuasively that a diaconal petition in the Great Euchology
of the White Monastery mentions "female deacons," which he takes to
mean "women who exercise the diaconate," but the actual presence of
such women at the White Monastery or anywhere else in Egypt is not
supported by other evidence—no epigraphical evidence naming Egyptian women as deacons or deaconesses and no mention of either in the
many works of Egyptian saints such as St. Athanasius the Great, St.
Cyril of Alexandria, or St. Isidore of Pelusium.[96] The Sahidic Coptic
version of the *Apostolic Constitutions* expressly forbids the ordination
of "female deacons."[97] There is also a mention of "female deacons" in

---

[92] Our source, the *Liber pontificalis*, mentions clergymen, noblemen, sena-
tors, soldiers, "et universo populo Romano cum sanctimonialibus et diaconis-
sis et nobilissimis matronis." See Martimort, 204.

[93] See Martimort, 202–209. According to Martimort, three ninth- or tenth-
century collections of canons explain Chalcedon's Canon 15 with the words,
"Diaconissa, id est abbatissa."

[94] See Karras (2004), 278.

[95] Karras, 274, reports this as the consensus accepted by "most scholars."Gryson, 34, 109, and Martimort, 76, agree with the consensus; Ugo Zanetti disagrees. See Zanetti, "Were There Deaconesses in Egypt?" *Women Deacons: Essays with Answers*, ed. Phyllis Zagano (Collegeville, Minn.: Liturgical
Press, 2016), 100–143.

[96] Zanetti, 165–167.

[97] See Zanetti, 166.

the fourth-century *Apostolic Church Order*, which is believed to have originated in Egypt, but this text also appears to forbid their ordination on the grounds that women have no place in the altar.[98] The fourth-century *Canons of Hippolytus*, which survives only in Arabic and is believed to have been written in Egypt, does not mention women deacons or deaconesses and expressly forbids the ordination of widows "because ordination is for men."[99]

Deaconesses were not ubiquitous even in the regions where they were known. No canon required their ordination or reserved for them alone the tasks traditionally associated with the order.[100] Even the *Didascalia* allowed that in the absence of a deaconess the anointing of women could be done by a laywoman or clergyman.[101] The question of need was therefore left to each bishop to decide, and it seems that over time more and more bishops decided that deaconesses were not needed.[102]

Even in Asia Minor, the order seems to have followed the empire's fortunes, peaking in the early sixth century and declining steadily

---

[98] The *Apostolic Church Order* is also known as the *Canones Ecclesiastici* and *Statutes of the Apostles*. Quasten (1950), 119, says it "seems to have been composed in Egypt, although there are some who think that it came from Syria." It includes a passage on women beginning with the saying, attributed to Andrew, "It is a good thing to set apart women to be made deacons" (Horner, 305) or "It would be useful, brothers, to institute a ministry for women" (Martimort, 87), but the rest of the passage is an argument against a ministry for women, ending with the exception "that they should help the needy" (Horner, 305) or "unless it is a ministry of comfort to those who are in need" (Martimort, 87).

[99] See Canon 9, *The Canons of Hippolytus*, ed. Paul Bradshaw, trans. Carol Bebawi (Nottingham: Grove Books Limited, 1987), 16.

[100] This includes the canons of the seven councils regarded as "ecumenical" by the Orthodox Church, plus the canons of the local councils and hierarchs and the 85 "Canons of the Apostles" endorsed by ecumenical council. It does not include the aforesaid Jacobite canon directing that deaconesses be ordained to head women's monasteries.

[101] *Didascalia* 15.3.12, Connolly, 70.

[102] The sixth- and seventh-century monk John Moschus tells the story of an archbishop in Palestine who wanted to ordain a deaconess to anoint a very beautiful young woman from Persia, but who did not do so "because the place did not permit it" (διὰ τὸ μὴ ἐπιδέχεσθαι τὸν τόπον). It is not clear whether "the place" meant that part of the country or the monastery where the woman had gone to be baptized, but the incident shows that other considerations sometimes trumped the supposed need for deaconesses. See Martimort, 132–133.

thereafter. Karras writes, "Especially outside the capital city of Constantinople and holy city of Jerusalem, there is almost no indication of a female diaconate beyond a seal and a few passing references emanating from Byzantine Italy in the liminal seventh and eighth centuries."[103]

Late in their history, deaconesses in Constantinople seem to have been known chiefly for their singing. Thus, about 1148, Anna Comnena writes of her father, Alexius I, who died in 1118, "For he arranged in the renovated Church of the Apostles to have men and women singers, in imitation of Solomon, for the work of deaconesses was also his concern."[104] Two generations later, around 1200, we have an eyewitness account by Anthony of Novgorod of a group of women he calls "Myrrhbearers" singing in the Great Church in Constantinople, at or near the place where the deaconesses were said to stand, but his use of the term "Myrrhbearers" may indicate that these female singers were no longer "deaconesses."[105]

That is certainly how Theodore Balsamon saw them. A deacon himself and a leading canonist who spent his entire life in Constantinople, dying there in 1199, perhaps during Anthony's visit, Balsamon twice writes that deaconesses are a thing of the past. First, in his commentary on Canon 15 of Chalcedon, he writes that deaconesses are no longer ordained, that some nuns are wrongly called "deaconesses," and that they have no access to the altar.[106] Then, in reply to a query from Patriarch Mark III of Alexandria, who was perplexed by the mention of deaconesses in the canons, Balsamon repeats the same three points, adding that the pseudo-deaconesses of his day are mostly just part of the assembly (ἐκκλησιάζουσαι δὲ τὰ πολλὰ) and mind the

---

[103] Karras (2004), 310.
[104] Anna Comnena, *Alexiad*, 15.7.8: "Κατέταξε γὰρ τῷ τῶν ἀποστόλων νεῷ ᾄδοντας καὶ ᾀδούσας κατὰ τὸν Σολομῶντα. Ἐπιμελὲς γὰρ καὶ τὸ τῶν διακονισσῶν πεποίηκεν ἔργον." https://el.wikisource.org/wiki/Ἀλεξιάς/ Βιβλίο_15, accessed August 20, 2016. Martimort, 171, cautions against relating the second clause to the first clause, but Karras suggests it. See Karras (2004), 276, n. 20.
[105] See Karras (2004), 283.
[106] Theodore Balsamon, *Scholia in Concilium Chalcedonense*, PG 137, 441C–D, quoted in Martimort, 171.

gynaeceum in church (τὴν γυναικωνῖτιν ἐκκλησιαστικῶς διορθού-μεναι).[107]

Remaining Questions

Using literary evidence alone, we can easily chart the trajectory of deaconesses in the regions where they were most common—from "minor clergy" in the fourth century, to "major clergy" in the sixth century, to "minor clergy" and then lay office before the twelfth century, and finally to defunct office by order of Patriarch Athanasius I of Constantinople in the first decade of the fourteenth century.[108] The dozen or so Byzantine euchologies with an ordination rite for deaconesses represent the apogee of this trajectory, the status of deaconesses in the imperial capital in the fifth or sixth century.[109]

But not the status of deaconesses everywhere or even anywhere at all times. Elsewhere the trajectory of deaconesses was much flatter, never rising above "minor clergy" in Italy, Sicily, and Gaul, and never existing at all in Egypt, Africa, Spain, Ireland, Britain, or Russia. This makes arguments in favor of ordaining deaconesses based on tradition very difficult, because the whole Church has never had a tradition of ordaining deaconesses, but the whole Church has had a longstanding tradition of *not* ordaining them.

To settle the issue one way or the other, we must answer two questions: Why did many parts of the Church never have deaconesses, and why did the parts of the Church that once had deaconesses stop having them? Only after answering both questions will we be able to decide whether the Church's reasons for not ordaining deaconesses do or do not still exist. The rest of this work will attempt to answer both questions, starting with the question of disappearance.

---

[107] Theodore Balsamon, *Responsa ad interrogationes Marci 35*, PG 138, 988A–B, in Martimort, 172.

[108] See Karras (2004), 276.

[109] The rite seems to have been already in existence in the early sixth century because that is when the Jacobite bishops mention the bestowal of an orar, although it is possible that that feature of the rite preceded other features. We cannot say how long the rite was in use because service books are notoriously conservative, often including customs abandoned centuries earlier. As it happens, none of the Byzantine euchologies containing a rite for the ordination of deaconesses can be positively dated after Patriarch Athanasius's *entalma* forbidding their appointment.

CHAPTER 2

What Changed? Church Needs, the Gender Order, or the Church Order?

Several factors have been proposed as possible contributors to the disappearance of the deaconess, including infant baptism, fear of gnosticism, fear of paganism, fear of heresy, the iconoclastic controversy, the growth of the minor male orders, Western influence, Islamic influence, and growing concern for ritual purity. These factors can be grouped into three categories of change: changes in church needs, changes in the gender order (normative sex roles), and changes in the church order (roles of clergy and laity).

Infant baptism stands out as the most obvious change in church needs affecting the order of deaconess. Assisting in the baptism of adult women was the original purpose of the order and the duty most often associated with it. With the nearly complete Christianization of many local populations and with infant baptism becoming standard practice among Christians, the need for a deaconess to assist in the baptism of women became a rare occasion. Two medieval texts blame infant baptism for the disappearance of deaconesses, the eleventh-century Jacobite *Book of Guidance* by Yahya ibn Jarir of Persia and a twelfth-century pontifical of Syrian patriarch known as Michael the Great.[110] Both of these works say that deaconesses are no longer ordained and both name infant baptism as the reason, although the *Book of Guidance* adds, "But there was another reason as well—namely, that

---

[110] Martimort, 166–167.

the queens penetrated into the sanctuary, and so permission was abolished."[111] The mention of "queens" is curious. It could mean uppity women who overstepped their bounds, like those condemned in Gaul for distributing Communion, or actual queens like St. Pulcheria, who thought it her right as empress to commune in the altar and took offense when Nestorius barred her way.[112]

Most modern scholars have accepted infant baptism as the leading factor, but not the only factor. The decline in frequent communion could also have been a factor, although only a slight one. The duty of carrying Communion to homebound women is much less attested and may not have been general practice, and the decline in frequent Communion and Communion at home began early, toward the end of the fourth century, just as deaconesses were reaching their heyday.[113] The need to honor rich patronesses and the wives of men becoming bishops may also have waned as the wealth of the empire diminished and more monks became bishops. But what of the other duties of deaconesses such as singing in church, minding the *gynaeceum*, tending to sick and needy women, and heading convents? Why were these duties not sufficient to maintain an order thought to have been apostolic? And why were the duties of deaconesses so limited in the first place, such that infant baptism could put deaconesses out of business?

To answer these questions, scholars have looked elsewhere, beyond presumed changes in the needs of the Church to the possibility of changes in the order of the Church or in its understanding of gender.

Changes in the Gender Order

Reading Scripture the Greek way whereby the female diaconate appears to have been apostolic, some scholars have assumed that its decline and demise represents a change in the Church's beliefs about proper sex roles. To explain the change, they have speculated on a

---

[111] Martimort, 166.
[112] We will return to this encounter in the final section. For more, see Nicholas P. Constas, "Weaving the Body of God," *Journal of Early Christian Studies* 3 (1995) 173–174, and Kenneth G. Holum, *Theodosian Empresses: Women and Imperial Dominion in Late Antiquity* (Berkeley: University of California Press, 1982), 152–155.
[113] Even in *The Testament of Our Lord*, one of the few sources to mention the practice, deaconesses carried Communion only to expectant mothers and only at Pascha.

number of factors supposed to have made Christians less tolerant of women clergy, but none of the suggested factors has been demonstrated to have had the supposed effect, and all suffer from a want of supporting evidence and not a little wishful thinking.

Kyriaki FitzGerald, for example, attributes to John Romanides and Roger Gryson the suggestion that Western resistance to deaconesses was, in FitzGerald's words, "a fear-based reaction" to paganism, Gnosticism, or Montanism, which made "the regional leadership understandably and increasingly gynekophobic in regards to ecclesial ministries."[114] She does not, however, provide any evidence to this effect, and she misrepresents Gryson's argument, which is not that fear of Montanism prompted bishops in Gaul to forbid what they had formerly allowed, but that they had always regarded clergywomen, in Gryson's words, as "an innovation in Gaul, an unprecedented superstition, an illicit ministry, which soiled the divine sacraments [such that] they needed no more explicit explanation to order these practices to cease without delay."[115] It must also be said that the orthodox were not always averse to accepting innovations originating among heretics. St. Ephrem of Syria, for example, is said to have organized a choir of virgins to compete with those of the heretics Bardesan and Harmodius.[116] We cannot therefore assume that the bishops of Gaul resisted deaconesses solely because they were an innovation of heretics. Something else must have made this particular innovation unacceptable.

Other factors have been suggested for the disappearance of deaconesses in the East. Karras notes the coincidence of the decline of the order with iconoclasm and wonders whether deaconesses suffered a loss of prestige on account of their involvement in the controversy, but she admits that there is no evidence of a connection.[117] FitzGerald suggests the influence of Roman Catholic and Protestant conceptions of

---

[114] FitzGerald only paraphrases comments allegedly made to her in private by Romanides. See Kyriaki Karidoyanes FitzGerald, *Women Deacons in the Orthodox Church: Called to Holiness and Ministry* (Brookline, Mass.: Holy Cross Orthodox Press, 1999), 136–137.

[115] Gryson, 106.

[116] Assemani's *Bibliotheca Orientalis*, in Johannes Quasten, *Music & Worship in Pagan & Christian Antiquity*, trans. Boniface Ramsey (Washington, DC: National Association of Pastoral Musicians, 1983), 79.

[117] Karras (2004), 310–311.

holy orders and femininity, but these influences came much later, after both the Great Schism and the disappearance of deaconesses in the East, and are therefore relevant only to Orthodox views of deaconesses in the late middle ages and modern era.[118] FitzGerald also wonders vaguely whether Islam "and its impact upon societal norms and theological reflection may also have been a factor in the decline of the practice of ordaining women as deacons." She does not elaborate, except to say that "Christian women who were active in a visible and public ministry may have proved to be a potential source of vulnerability" under Muslim rule.[119] But what public ministry did deaconesses perform that would have been visible to Muslims? And what Muslim norms did Christians imitate?[120] The influence of Islam on the status of women among the Byzantines is often assumed by modern Westerners, but evidence for it before deaconesses disappeared is not to be had. Arab women were always more extreme in their modesty, covering not just their heads but their faces, and long before the appearance of Islam *Christian* women were obliged by *Christian* custom to dress as modestly as most Muslim women do today.[121] Judging by both canon law

---

[118] FitzGerald, 141–143.

[119] FitzGerald, 140.

[120] Some historians have argued that Islam contributed to Christian iconoclasm. After all, the emperor Leo III (717–741) was said in his day to be "Saracen-minded" (σαρακηνόφρων) on account of his opposition to icons and usury. See Ostrogorsky, 161. But the Byzantines successfully resisted such influence, keeping both icons and usury. The Church in the East prohibited clergymen from lending at interest but not laymen (Canon 44 of the 85 Apostolic Canons, Canon 17 of the First Ecumenical Council, Canon 10 of the Council *in Trullo*, Canon 4 of Laodicea, Canon 14 of Basil the Great), and Christians in the East continued to practice usury throughout Byzantine history, regulated by civil law limiting interest to between 4 and 12 percent, depending upon the lender and the purpose. Two emperors, Nicephorus I and Basil I, attempted to ban usury by private citizens, but their intent was to monopolize lending by the imperial treasury, not to proscribe it entirely. The Byzantine Empire was, after all, a commercial commonwealth, dependent for its existence upon investment and trade. See George Ostrogorsky, *History of the Byzantine State* (New Brunswick, N.J.: Rutgers University Press, 1969), 189–190.

[121] Commenting in the early third century on the Apostle Paul's requirement for women to cover their head in 1 Cor. 11:2–16, Tertullian shames Christians for being outdone by Arabs, saying, "Arabia's heathen females will be your judges, who cover not only the head, but the face also, so entirely, that they are content, with one eye free, to enjoy rather half the light than to prostitute the entire face." *On the Veiling of Virgins*, PL 2, 912A–B, ANF 4, 37.

and civil law on sex and marriage, the Byzantines remained quite distinctly Christian and Roman to the end of the empire. Western Christians might have learned a thing or two from Muslims, but Eastern Christians saw little in Islam worth imitating.[122]

Both FitzGerald and Karras give weight to the influence of the late Byzantine concern for ritual purity, with Karras writing that "the most likely answer [for both the beginning of the decline of the order in the seventh century and the disappearance of the order before the late twelfth century] is the introduction into the Byzantine Church beginning in the late seventh century of severe liturgical restrictions on menstruating women."[123] The introduction she seems to have in mind is Canon 2 of the Council *in Trullo* in 692, which summarily approves many ancient canons, including the third-century canons of St. Dionysius of Alexandria, which bar menstruating women from approaching the altar and touching the Holy Gifts, and the fourth-century canons of St. Timothy of Alexandria, which bar menstruating women from receiving Holy Communion.[124]

Karras's bases for focusing on the Council *in Trullo* are two comments made five centuries later by Theodore Balsamon. The first is from Balsamon's answer to Patriarch Mark III of Alexandria, mentioned above, in which the canonist says of deaconesses that "the impurity of their menstrual periods dictated their separation from the divine and holy sanctuary."[125] The second is from Balsamon's commentary on Canon 15 of Chalcedon, mentioned above, in which he says that "there is a law that prohibits women from entering the sanctuary. How then could a woman, who does not even have the right to

---

[122] After a lengthy survey of Byzantine writing about Islam, Stefano Nikolaou concludes, "The cultural achievements of Islam did not impress the Byzantines whatsoever. Due to their tradition of Classical scholarship, direct descent from the Ancient Greeks, and the idea that they were a continuation of the Roman Empire, the Byzantines maintained their cultural and ethical superiority through the period of cultural contact." See Nikolaou's unpublished dissertation entitled "A Survey of Byzantine Responses to Islam," Australian Catholic University, 2007, http://www.answering-islam.org/history/byzantine_responses.html, accessed August 23, 2016.

[123] Karras (2004), 311–314.

[124] The canons in question are Canon 2 of St. Dionysius and Question 7 of St. Timothy.

[125] Theodore Balsamon, *Responsa ad interrogationes Marci 35*, PG 138, 988A–B, in Martimort, 172.

approach the altar, possibly exercise the office of deacon?"[126] To these opinions, both Karras and FitzGerald add a comment a century and a half later by the canonist Matthew Blastares that unnamed persons in the past (presumably Balsamon) attributed the separation of deaconesses from the altar (and presumably the decline of the order) to menstruation.[127] But there are several problems with this theory:

1. Both Balsamon and Blastares were writing well after the end of the order, with no personal experience of·deaconesses. They were as dependent as we are on literary evidence, appear to know less than we do about the subject, and therefore testify more to the thinking of their own age than to the thinking behind the decline of the order of deaconesses over several preceding centuries.

2. Balsamon is the only authority to connect menstruation to the decline of the female diaconate, and he appears to do so out of ignorance. He seems unaware that deaconesses assisted in baptism, performed other duties outside the altar, or were defined in any way differently from deacons, and so he assumes that, because they are "deacons," they served in the altar before being excluded from it.

3. Blastares, in contrast, is aware that deaconesses were said to have assisted in baptism and does not buy Balsamon's menstruation argument, citing other reasons for excluding women from the altar. After stating Balsamon's opinion and then conceding that women were sometimes permitted to enter the altar, he writes, "However, it does not appear plausible to me that a woman became a deacon of the Sacred and Bloodless Sacrifice, as there is no sound reason why women, who are not permitted to teach in public, should be raised to the rank of the diaconate, whose work is to purify orally those unbelievers that come forward for baptism."[128]

---

[126] Theodore Balsamon, *Scholia in Concilium Chalcedonense*, PG 137 441C–D, quoted in Martimort, 171.

[127] Matthew Blastares, *Syntagma, littera Gamma*, PG 144 1173–1176.

[128] Matthew Blastares, *Syntagma, littera Gamma*, PG 144, 1173D, translated by Patrick Demetrios Viscuso, *Sexuality, Marriage, and Celibacy in Byzantine Law: The Alphabetical Collection of Matthew Blastares* (Brookline, Mass.: Holy Cross Orthodox Press, 2008), 111. Cf. Martimort, 173. Viscuso and Karras (2004), 314, understand Blastares to say, with Balsamon, that menstruation was the reason deaconesses are no longer ordained, but this

4. Neither the concern for ritual impurity nor the exclusion of women from the altar were new developments in the late seventh century. Both, in fact, pre-dated the heyday of the female diaconate. In addition to the canons of Sts. Dionysius and Timothy of Alexandria, Canon 44 of the Council of Laodicea, circa 364, barred women from the altar for no stated reason, and the prayer said over a deaconess in the fourth-century *Apostolic Constitutions* includes a petition to "cleanse her from all filthiness of flesh and spirit" (cf. 2 Cor. 7:1), which does not appear in the prayers said over male clerics, and which Paul Bradshaw takes to be a reference to menstruation.[129]

5. Byzantine concern for ritual impurity did intensify over time, but this change likely had less to do with the summary approval of ancient canons in 692 than with the burgeoning veneration of the Theotokos after the Third Ecumenical Council in Ephesus in 431, in particular the increasing popularity and liturgical use of the *Protoevangelium of James*, which explains Mary's betrothal to Joseph as a way to get her out of the Temple before she reaches puberty, as well as the attention given the purification of Mary in the celebration of the Meeting of our Lord in the Temple (February 2), a feast known in the West until modern times as the Purification of the Blessed Virgin Mary.[130]

6. Deaconesses assisted in the altar only in convents and only when there were no men to assist. As that need would have persisted, we might expect that the concern for ritual impurity would have had the opposite effect. Instead of being a reason to do away

---

confounds the logic of Blastares's commentary by mistaking his statement of Balsamon's opinion for a statement of his own opinion. The passage only makes sense if we understand Blastares to be saying (a) some authorities say women assisted at baptism, (b) others say they assisted in the altar but were later forbidden to do so on account of menstruation, but (c) although women were allowed at times to enter the altar, "it does not appear plausible to me" that they ever assisted in the altar because women are not allowed to teach and so cannot be deacons. (The example he cites of a woman entering the altar is St. Gorgonia, St. Gregory the Theologian's sister, who dared to enter the altar, touch the Holy Table, and consume the Holy Gifts in a furtive, late-night plea for healing. Homily 8, PG 35, 789–817)

[129] Bradshaw (1990), 86.

[130] See Hugh Wybrew, *Orthodox Feasts of Jesus Christ and the Virgin Mary* (Crestwood, N.Y.: St. Vladimir Seminary Press, 2000), 19–20.

with deaconesses, it would have been a reason to make older women deaconesses as a way of certifying their safety for service in the altar. After all, Justinian's minimum age of 50 would have ensured that most deaconesses were beyond the age of menstruation.[131]

With this in mind, it seems altogether unlikely that concern for ritual purity was the driving force behind the decline of an order believed to be apostolic. It seems rather more imaginable that it was used as an excuse to curb a sometimes bothersome order for which clergymen saw no important purpose. In Balsamon's case, however, it seems only to have been an improvised answer offered in ignorance.

Without an explanation of the change in attitude among Byzantine Christians toward deaconesses, advocates of reviving the order leave us with two conflicting images: At times, the Byzantines are presented as so sexually egalitarian that they ordained women as "deacons" to perform a "visible and public ministry" as members of the "major clergy"; at other times, they are alleged to have been so burdened with "gynekophobic" cultural baggage that they wouldn't let deaconesses do much and eventually did away with them. The underlying assumption is that the Church was originally more egalitarian than it later became, but our inability to say when and how this happened calls that assumption into question.[132]

Did the Gender Order Change?

Most research on deaconesses has been narrowly focused on literary references to deaconesses, widows, virgins, and abbesses, with little attention paid to the broader issue of Christian belief about the man and the woman. This has left researchers without a firm basis from which to evaluate the very limited and often-ambiguous evidence of deaconesses, with the result that appraisals of the deaconess's place

---

[131] Age at menopause varies from person to person and culture to culture, but in the U.S. today, 50 is the average age of onset. See T.A. Takahashi, et al., "Menopause," *Medical Clinics of North America*, 99.3 (May 2015) 521–534.
[132] Marucci's assumptions about apostolic egalitarianism are revealed when he writes, 12, against all evidence, "The fact that a woman performs such 'ministry' cannot appear *a priori* impossible for those who bear in mind the gender climate of equality of the sexes that emerges in the New Testament."

within the Church are sometimes based on anachronistic assumptions about what early Christians considered appropriate.

For example, it is often stated as fact that women prophesied (i.e., preached) in the public assemblies of the Church in the apostolic era.[133] The basis for this assertion is a modern reading of two verses of Holy Scripture: Acts 21:9, which says that the daughters of Philip prophesied, and 1 Corinthians 11:5, in which the Apostle Paul says that women are to cover their heads when they pray or prophesy. The basis for the modern reading of these verses is the modern assumption that prophecy is a liturgical act performed in a public assembly of the Church. This assumption is no doubt influenced by 1 Corinthians 14, in which Paul argues in favor of prophesying over speaking in tongues for the sake of edifying others "when you come together." In chapter 14, the Apostle refers unambiguously to the setting being *in church* at least five times—verses 19, 23, 26, 28, and 35.[134] The last of these five verses concerns women, whom the Apostle forbids to speak in church, even to ask questions, "for it is a shame for a woman to speak in church."

But St. Paul's comments in 1 Corinthians on public worship do not begin until *after* his brief lesson on honoring one's "head" in 1 Corinthians 11, which begins with a word of praise in verse 2 ("Now I praise you, brethren, that ye remember me in all things and keep the ordinances as I delivered them to you") and ends with an appeal to universal church custom in verse 16.[135] Nowhere in this lesson does the Apostle mention church as the setting of the prayer or prophecy. Only when he has finished his lesson on head-covering does he take up the issue of how to behave in church, with verse 17 ("Now in this that I declare unto you I praise you not, that ye come together not for the better, but

---

[133] For example, Behr-Sigel, 117, writes: "Paul's letters show that women prayed and 'prophesied' in the first Christian assemblies (1 Cor. 11:4)."

[134] Five more verses in chapter 14 (4, 5, 12, 33, 34) mention "church" or "churches," but these could be understood to mean the Church or local churches and not the setting "in church" (ἐν ἐκκλησίᾳ).

[135] Note the structure of chapter 11: First, in verse 2, St. Paul says, "I praise you," then, in verse 17, he says, "I praise you not." Many exegetes, ancient and modern, have assumed that the Corinthians were not keeping the custom of head-covering of which the Apostle speaks, but nowhere in the letter does Paul actually accuse them of this fault, and when he turns from praising to praising not, the fault he mentions "first of all" is not bareheaded women but "divisions among you."

for the worse.") How, then, can his mention of women prophesying in chapter 11 constitute an exception to his emphatic prohibition on women speaking in church in chapter 14? Is private prophecy not possible?

Montanists and other heretical sects certainly did assume prophecy to be an exception to the silence required of women, but no ancient orthodox authority did.[136] Origen treats the issue scornfully, writing, "Even if it is granted to a woman to prophesy and show the sign of prophecy, she is nevertheless not permitted to speak in an assembly." Of the daughters of Philip, he writes, "at least they did not speak in the assemblies, for we do not find this fact in the Acts of the Apostles." He ends his argument with the words, "'A women [prophesying] in an assembly': clearly this abuse is denounced as improper—an abuse for which the entire assembly is responsible."[137]

St. John Chrysostom speaks of the "unseasonable boldness" of women who dared to speak in church, saying, "because they supposed this to be an ornament to them, I mean their speaking in public, again he brings round the discourse to the opposite point, saying, 'For it is shameful for a woman to speak in the church.'"[138] Elsewhere he says, "To such a degree should women be silent that they are not allowed to speak not only about worldly matters, but not even about spiritual things, in the church. This is order, this is modesty, this will adorn her

---

[136] St. Irenaeus of Lyon is sometimes cited in support of women prophesying in church, based on his mention of "men and women in the Church prophesying" (*viros et mulieres in Ecclesia prophetantes*), but these words are part of an argument against Montanism, and Irenaeus's point is not that men and women prophesied *in church*, but that the gift of prophecy was already given to the Church at Pentecost, so Montanists sin against the Holy Spirit by claiming a "new outpouring." See St. Irenaeus, *Adv. Her.* 3.11; PG 7, 891A.
[137] Fragment 74 on 1 Corinthians, in Gryson, 28–29; JTS 10, 41–42. Origen names four Old Testament women whom he says prophesied privately but not publicly: Deborah, Huldah, Aaron's sister Miriam, and Phanuel's daughter Hannah, to which we might add Noadiah and the wife of the prophet Isaiah.
[138] St. John Chrysostom, Homily 37 on 1 Corinthians, PG 61, 315–316, NPNF1 12, 222.

more than any garments."[139] Theodoret of Cyrus is even more explicit with regard to prophecy, writing of 1 Corinthians 14:

> Since, however, not only men but also women enjoyed grace—God himself foretelling it also through the prophet Joel, "I shall pour out my spirit upon all flesh, and your sons and your daughters will prophesy" [Joel 2:28]—he had to regulate for the latter as well: "Let your women keep silent in the churches: their role is not to speak but to be subject, as the Law also says." [1 Cor. 14:34] God said to Eve, "Your yearning is for your husband, and in turn he will have dominion over you." [Gen. 3:16][140]

Pelagius writes of 1 Corinthians 11:5 that women may prophesy only "among her sex and at home" (*in suo sexu et in domo*).[141] He is equally emphatic that women may not speak in public or teach men in his comments on 1 Corinthians 14: 34–35, 1 Timothy 3:11, and Titus 2:4.[142] There is also an anonymous fourth-century anti-Montanist dialogue in which the "Orthodox" character says:

> We do not reject the prophesies of women. Blessed Mary prophesied when she said: "Henceforth all generations shall call me blessed." And as you yourself say, Philip had daughters who prophesied, and Mary, the sister of Aaron, prophesied. But we do not permit women to speak in the assemblies, nor to have authority over men.[143]

Even those who say today that women did prophesy in church in Paul's day grant that this freedom did not last long, so if a change in the gender order did occur within the Church, it occurred very early, in first

---

[139] St. John Chrysostom, Homily 9 on 1 Timothy, PG 62, 543–544, NPNF1 13, 435.

[140] Theodoret of Cyrus, Commentary on 1 Corinthians, PG 82 347A, in *Commentary on the Letters of St. Paul*, trans. Robert Charles Hill (Brookline, Mass.: Holy Cross Orthodox Press, 2001), 223.

[141] Pelagius, Commentary on 1 Corinthians, PLS 1, 1214.

[142] Pelagius, Commentary on 1 Corinthians, PLS 1, 1214; Commentary on 1 Timothy, PLS 1, 1349; and Commentary on Titus, PLS 1, 1370.

[143] See Gryson, 76.

or second century. Yet we have no account of any woman ever standing up to preach in an orthodox assembly and no example of any orthodox Father ever torturing the text of 1 Corinthians to justify women preaching in church in the apostolic era.[144] No Father says, "Women must remain silent, but they may prophesy in the assembly." Instead, they say, "Women may prophesy, but they must remain silent in the assembly."

Karras, nevertheless, argues that women were allowed to prophesy in church in the apostolic era—they just weren't allowed to ask questions. The proof, she says, is 1 Corinthians 11:5, which she assumes refers to "public preaching, particularly on moral issues."[145] On the subject of deaconesses, she demonstrates a similar tendency to exaggerate their liturgical role without due regard for the historical record. She writes, for instance, "By the late middle Byzantine period, the liturgical function of chanting appears to have become one of the ministries of female deacons not only in women's monasteries but also in the Great Church."[146]

Now, the English word *chanting* can mean three things to the Orthodox of today: It can mean simply "singing," or it can mean intoning a text without much melodic elaboration (sometimes called "plainchanting"), or it can mean performing the duties of a cantor or canonarch—duties that in ancient times were reserved for clerics by Canon 15 of Laodicea and Canon 33 of the Council *in Trullo*.[147] Karras notes that "chanting" was a clerical duty; she also often refers to deaconesses as "chanters" and strongly prefers "chanting" over "singing" when

---

[144] The only approved public preaching of women occurred at trial, when women boldly defended the Faith before their persecutors.
[145] Karras (2005), 98, writes that "the context of 1 Corinthians 14:34 clearly indicates that the 'speaking' that was prohibited to women was of the question-and-answer variety." Behr-Sigel, 117, also assumes the women prophesied in the apostolic era.
[146] Karras (2004), 283.
[147] Laodicea 15 says, "No others shall sing in the Church, save only the canonical singers, who go up into the ambo and sing from a book." The ancient epitome reads, "No one should ascend the ambo unless he is tonsured." NPNF2 14, 132. Canon 33 of *Trullo* forbids anyone to "read in the ambo, according to the order of those enrolled in the clergy, unless such a one has received the priestly tonsure." NPNF2 14, 381.

speaking of deaconesses.[148] Her readers might therefore be forgiven for understanding her to mean that deaconesses were allowed to ascend the ambo in the midst of the Great Church to lead the singing, sing solo, or chant Scripture.

Women did, of course, sing in church as members of the congregation and sometimes also as choirs of consecrated virgins, deaconesses, or "Myrrhbearers" (per Anthony of Novgorod). St. Ambrose of Milan writes, "The Apostle commands women to be silent in the church, but they may sing the psalms; this is fitting for every age and for both sexes."[149] Nuns also acted as readers and chanters in convents, and four nuns earned remembrance as hymnographers, but we have no record of women receiving the "priestly tonsure" required by Canon 33 of the Council *in Trullo* to be ranked among the clergy as readers or chanters, and it is only among heretics that we hear of women as individuals taking leading roles in the singing of cathedral or parish churches.[150]

In the later fourth century, we begin to hear calls for women not to sing in church. It is not always possible to tell whether these calls mean women singing among the people or the singing of individual women as readers or chanters. St. Jerome seems to mean the latter when he relates singing to both reading and teaching in an attack on the Pelagians:

---

[148] For a mention of "singing" by deaconesses, see Karras (2004), 284; for mentions of "chanting" by deaconesses or of deaconesses serving as "chanters," see Karras (2004), 276, 283, 284, 285, 287, 309, and 311.
[149] St. Ambrose of Milan, *Enarratio in Psalmum 1*, PL 14, 925A, in Quasten (1973), 78.
[150] The four were Cassia (variously Kassia, Kassiane, Cassiane), Theodosia, and Thekla of the ninth century and Palaiologina of the fourteenth century. See Eva Catafygiotu Topping, *Sacred Songs: Studies in Byzantine Hymnography* (Minneapolis, Minn.: Light & Life Publishing, 1997), 29–42. Cassia is now honored as a saint (Sept. 7). In the Arabic and Ethiopic versions of the so-called *Apostolic Church Order*, it is said that "concerning deaconesses, subdeaconesses, and lectresses, we have already spoken," but this is likely a mistranslation from the Coptic version, which speaks of "subdeacons, readers, and women deacons," which explains why the text makes no other mention of lectresses or subdeaconesses. See Martimort, 92–93, who quotes J.M. Hanssens explaining the mistranslation in *La liturgie d'Hippolyte* (I), OCA 155 (Rome, 1959), 113.

Who does not know that women should sing the praises of the Lord—in their own chambers, far removed from the meetings of men and the assemblies of the multitude? But you permit what is not permissible, namely, that they do what should be performed by them secretly and without any witnesses as though they were lawfully constituted teachers.[151]

Other voices clearly forbid all singing in church by women. The fourth-century pseudoepigraphic *Didascalia CCCXVIII Patrum Nicaenorum* says, "Women are ordered not to speak in church, not even softly, nor may they sing along or take part in the responses, but they should only be silent and pray to God."[152] Johannes Quasten blames the opposition to women's singing on the popularity of women's choirs among Gnostics and heretics such as Montanists, Paulianists, and Marcionites, but this begs the question of why the orthodox considered the practice of these heretics inappropriate. St. Isidore of Pelusium in Egypt gives us a clue in a letter of the early fifth century, in which he complains that in city churches people were taking too much pleasure in public worship and turning churches into theaters:

The Apostles of the Lord, being keen to control and even suppress troublesome talkativeness in the assemblies, offering themselves to us as masters of humility and gravity, by wise counsel permitted women to sing among themselves. Nevertheless, though all of their divine examples are to the contrary, this led in most cases to laxity and an occasion for sin because the women were not moved with great compunction from the divine hymns, but instead, misusing the charm of singing to provoke and excite desires, for no reason at all, they considered the singing to be more outstanding than theatrical choruses. It is therefore worthwhile, if only because it is pleasing

---

[151] St. Jerome, *Dialogus Adversus Pelagianos*, PL 23, 519A–B, in Johannes Quasten, *Music & Worship in Pagan & Christian Antiquity*, trans. Boniface Ramsey (Washington, DC: National Association of Pastoral Musicians, 1983), 82. The connection between reading and teaching is evident in two English words, *lecture* and *lesson*, both of which derive from the Latin *legere*, meaning "to read." In the Anglican tradition, the readings of Scripture are still called "lessons."

[152] See Quasten (1983), 81.

to God, to seek to forbid it, as we wish singing to be for the edification of all; and considering how their misuse of singing was the same as misusing Christ for the profit of shopkeepers and converting divine grace to ruin as wages, let them not sing in church, and let them stay in the city.[153]

St. Isidore was a Desert Father, and his words ring with monastic rigor, but even the many Fathers who approved of women singing in church took very seriously the words of the Apostle Paul concerning the modesty required of women in both dress and demeanor. The rule on silence in church was routinely included in the briefest summaries of appropriate behavior for women. St. Cyprian of Carthage's Rule 46, St. Cyril of Jerusalem's instructions for catechumens, St Basil the Great's Rule 73, and Canon 70 of the Council *in Trullo* all require silence of women in church, citing the Apostle Paul as their authority.[154] St. Ambrose of Milan recommends silence for virgins:

I should prefer, therefore, that conversation should rather be wanting to a virgin, than abound. For if women are bidden to keep silence in churches, even about divine things, and to ask their husbands at home, what do we think should be the caution of virgins, in whom modesty adorns their age, and silence commends their modesty?[155]

Likewise, St. Basil writes concerning monastics that "in women's life more and greater modesty is required, as regards the virtues of poverty

---

[153] St. Isidore of Pelusium, Epistle 1.90, PG 78 243–246.
[154] Cf. 1 Cor. 14:34–35 and 1 Tim. 2:11–15. St. Basil, *Moralia*, Rule 73, PG 32, 853B; St. Cyril of Jerusalem writes of those waiting to be baptized: "Further, let the men when sitting have a useful book; and let one read, and another listen. And if there be no book, let one pray, and another speak something useful. And again let the party of young women sit together in like manner, either singing or reading quietly, so that their lips speak, but others' ears catch not the sound: *for I suffer not a woman to speak in the Church.* And let the married woman also follow the same example, and pray; and let her lips move, but her voice be unheard . . ." St. Cyril of Jerusalem, *Procatechesis*, PG 33, 356A–B, NPNF2 7, 4.
[155] St. Ambrose of Milan, *On Virgins*, PL 16, 222C, NPNF2 10, 382–383.

and quiet and obedience and sisterly love."[156] St. Gregory the Theologian praises both his sister and his mother for their silence. Of his mother, St. Nonna, he writes that "in the holy assemblies, or places, her voice was never to be heard except in the necessary responses of the service."[157] Of his sister, St. Gorgonia, he writes:

> What more sagacious than her words? What more prudent than her silence? Having mentioned silence, I will proceed to that which was most characteristic of her, most becoming to women, and most serviceable to these times. Who had a fuller knowledge of the things of God, both from the Divine oracles, and from her own understanding? But who was less ready to speak, confining herself within the due limits of women?[158]

St. Jerome credits St. Marcella of Rome with the same modesty:

> . . . when she answered questions she gave her own opinion not as her own but as from me or someone else, thus admitting that what she taught she had herself learned from others. For she knew that the Apostle had said: "I suffer not a woman to teach," and she would not seem to inflict a wrong upon the male sex.[159]

We see in the quotations above that the rule on silence was not merely a check on the talkativeness of women. The Fathers' main concern was to preserve the gender order they had inherited from the Apostles, to which the Scriptures bore witness. The Apostle Paul prescribes silence for women on two occasions (1 Cor. 14:34–35 and 1 Tim. 2:11–15), and both times he relates silence to the subjection of the woman to the man. Twice also the Apostle bases this subjection on both the Creation and the Fall (1 Cor. 11:8–9 and 1 Tim. 2:13–14). The gender order is

---

[156] St. Basil the Great, Sermon 70, PG 31, 888A, in *The Ascetic Works of Saint Basil*, trans. W.K.L. Clarke (London: Society for Promoting Christian Knowledge), 143–144.
[157] St. Gregory the Theologian, Oration 18, PG 35, 996B, NPNF2 7, 257.
[158] St. Gregory the Theologian, Oration 8, PG 35, 802B, NPNF2 7, 241.
[159] St. Jerome, Letter 127, PL 22, 1091–1092, NPNF2 6, 255–256.

therefore both natural and economic, "since," says St. Irenaeus, "both nature and the law place the female under subjection."[160]

Without exception, the Fathers followed the Apostle. "For with us indeed the woman is reasonably subjected to the man," says Chrysostom, "since equality of honor causeth contention."[161] This subjection applied not just to married couples but to the sexes generally. Chrysostom even applied it to children, "since among the children the female doth not possess equal sway."[162] No sainted Father of the Orthodox Church challenged this teaching. Even St. Maximus the Confessor, who named "male and female" as the first of five "divisions" to be overcome before creation can be re-united with God, did not challenge the gender order of his day.[163] How could he? All those who did were condemned as heretics: Montanists, Eustathians, Antidicomarianites, Collyridians, and Quintillianists. Of the last, St. Epiphanius writes: "They have women bishops, presbyters, and the rest; they say that none of this makes any difference because 'in Christ Jesus there is neither male nor female.'" He then quotes Genesis 3:16, 1 Corinthians 11:8, 1 Timothy 2:12, and 1 Timothy 2:14 before exclaiming: "What prolific error there is in this world! And now that I have squashed a toothless, witless serpent like a gecko, I shall pass this sect by, beloved, and go on to the rest, calling upon God as the help of my lowliness, and for the fulfillment of my promise."[164]

This is the often ignored background of consistent Christian tradition, based on explicit apostolic teaching preserved in Holy Scripture, that easily explains not only why deaconesses were so limited where they did exist, but also why they were strongly resisted elsewhere and why they eventually ceased to exist everywhere. Ordaining

---

[160] St. Irenaeus of Lyon, Fragment 33, PG 7, 1245C: "γὰρ καὶ ἡ φύσις καὶ ὁ νόμος ὑποτάττει τὸ θῆλυ."
[161] St. John Chrysostom, Homily 26 on 1 Corinthians, PG 61, 215, NPNF1 12, 150.
[162] St. John Chrysostom, Homily 34 on 1 Corinthians, PG 61, 290, NPNF1 12, 204.
[163] Difficulty 41, PG 91, 1303–1314. For a thorough analysis of St. Maximus's view of male and female and how it does and does not fit within Christian tradition, see Brian Patrick Mitchell, *Origen's Revenge: The Greek and Hebrew Roots of Christian Thinking on Male and Female*, forthcoming from Pickwick Publications in 2021.
[164] St. Epiphanius, *Adv. Haer.*, PG 41, 881, in *Panarion,* trans. Williams, Vol. 2, 21–23.

women as deaconesses and ranking them among the clergy violated the natural and economic order by placing women over men in the hierarchy of the Church. Forced to tolerate the practice because people assumed it to be apostolic, the Fathers of the Church did much to discourage it, through strict limits on the duties and honors of deaconesses, a requirement for celibacy, a high minimum age, a ban on women chanting, a ban on women in the altar, a ban on the appointment of female presidents or *presbytides*, fewer and fewer ordinations of deaconesses, and finally a ban on such ordinations.[165]

Pietro Sorci as much as admits this when he writes that, "given the attachment to tradition concerning ministry, if Churches had had the slightest suspicion that the female diaconate was not founded in apostolic practice they would have never, ever, introduced such an innovation, which was sharply opposed to the surrounding culture and the heritage of Judaism."[166] In other words: But for the belief that Phoebe was a deaconess, the Church never would have had deaconesses.

This is telling admission. Sorci is saying that the practice of ordaining deaconesses was inconsistent with what ancient Christians believed about gender. The irony is that he says this to argue that deaconesses must be apostolic or the Church would not have had them—an argument that depends entirely upon his unsupported assertion that resistance to deaconesses stemmed from external influences, secular and Jewish, and not from an apostolic understanding of gender. He would have us believe that a shift from a more egalitarian apostolic regard for gender to a less egalitarian patristic regard for gender

---

[165] Canon 11 of the Council of Laodicea (ca. 364) states: "*Presbytides*, as they are called, or female presidents, are not to be appointed in the Church." NPNF2 14, 130. Who these *presbytides* were is not known, although they appear to have been widows or deaconesses who overstepped their bounds. Balsamon writes: "In old days, certain venerable women [*presbytides*] sat in catholic churches, and took care that the other women kept good and modest order. But from their habit of using improperly that which was proper, either through their arrogance or through their base self-seeking, scandal arose. Therefore the Fathers prohibited the existence in the Church thereafter of any more such women as are called *presbytides* or presidents." He goes on to say that no one may object to one woman presiding over other women in a monastery of women, "But for a woman to teach in a catholic church, where a multitude of men is gathered together, and women of different opinions, is, in the highest degree, indecorous and pernicious." NPNF2 14, 130.
[166] Sorci, 93.

inhibited "the continuation and evolution of the female diaconate."[167] Yet such a shift cannot be demonstrated without assuming that deaconesses were apostolic and that resistance to them was not.

What *can* be demonstrated is the evolution of offices within the Church away from reliance on un-ordained individuals exercising distinct spiritual gifts, toward greater reliance on ordained ministers with delegated authority ranked hierarchically according to their distinct sacramental roles. This evolution is also often ignored in discourses on deaconesses, yet it also helps explain why deaconesses were so limited where they did exist, why they were strongly resisted elsewhere, and why they eventually ceased to exist everywhere. This is the last piece of our puzzle, which we will now briefly outline.

---

[167] Immediately after blaming "the surrounding culture and the heritage of Judaism" for the Church accepting deaconesses only because they were apostolic, Sorci, 93, writes, "On the contrary, it is likely that such a mentality, together with the fact that female ministry was claimed by heterodox sects as menacing not only the orthodox faith but even the constitution of the Church, represented an obstacle to the continuation and evolution of the female diaconate."

CHAPTER 3

Changes in the Church Order

There are three aspects of church order that have varied over time in relation to each other, almost as overlapping phases in the Church's early centuries. First, there is the *organic* Church, in which members relate to each other and the world as interdependent members of a body, the Body of Christ, participating in various mutually supportive ministries according to the gifts given them by the Holy Spirit. Second, there is the *administrative* Church, staffed by officers given charge of various matters and exercising authority over others in those matters. Third, there is the *hierarchic* Church, which is a ranking order based on strictly defined sacramental roles by which those who are higher in the hierarchy purify, illumine, and perfect those who are lower in the hierarchy. All of these aspects inform our present understanding of sacramental ordination and what it means today to be a bishop, priest, or deacon in the Church.

The Organic Church

In chapter 12 of his first epistle to the Corinthians, the Apostle Paul likens the Church to a human body, whose many members are organically related by their shared life and interdependent work. The Corinthians had made the mistake of coveting the gift of tongues, thinking that speaking in tongues gave evidence of inspiration and greater godliness. St. Paul used the analogy of the body to explain that godliness does not exclude diversity. There are within the Church "differences of administrations," "diversities of operations," and "diversities of gifts" including wisdom, knowledge, faith, healing, miracles, discernment, tongues, and interpretation (1 Cor. 12:4–10, cf. Rom. 12:4–8). There are also many offices, "first apostles, secondarily prophets, thirdly teachers, after that miracles, then gifts of healings, helps, governments, diversities of tongues" (1 Cor. 12:28). Elsewhere, he writes that Christ "gave some, apostles; and some, prophets; and some, evangelists; and some, pastors and teachers, for the perfecting of the saints, for the work of the ministry, for the edifying of the body of Christ" (Eph. 4:11–12).

There is therefore an order to the body, but it is not a strictly hierarchical order. Apostles come first and prophets after them, but the order of all the rest is less precise, and nowhere does the Apostle relate one's place within the body to one's godliness. Instead, he stresses that those who *seem* weaker (δοκοῦντα ἀσθενέστερα) are no less important to the body (1 Cor. 12:22) and that those who *seem* less honorable (δοκοῦμεν ἀτιμότερα) deserve greater honor (1 Cor. 12:23). He then urges the Corinthians toward the thing most needful for all, the "more excellent way" of love (1 Cor. 12:31). In love, all can excel, no matter what their rank or their office or their gifts.

Noticeably absent from the Apostle's lists of offices are bishops, presbyters, and deacons. These are ranks rather than functions and are not clearly defined in the New Testament, which speaks sometimes of "apostles and presbyters" (Acts 15:2, 4, 6, 22, 23, and 16:4) and sometimes of "bishops and deacons" (Phil. 1:1, 1 Tim. 3), never mentioning apostles or presbyters with bishops or deacons.[168] Other early Christian texts follow the New Testament in pairing bishops and deacons, employing *presbyters* either not at all, as in the *Didache*, or as a general term for leading men, as in 1 Clement and *The Shepherd of Hermas*. The *Didache* associates bishops and deacons with prophecy and teaching, but it has much more to say about prophets and teachers, mentioning bishops and deacons just once—an indication of the importance of the charismatic offices in the first-century Church.[169]

---

[168] The Apostles Peter and John both call themselves "elders" (1 Peter 5:1, 2 John 1:1, 3 John 1:1), and, as noted earlier, the Apostle Paul calls himself a "deacon" several times (1 Cor. 3:5; 2 Cor. 3:6, 6:4; Eph. 3:7; Col. 1:23, 25).

[169] The *Didache*: "Appoint, therefore, for yourselves, bishops and deacons worthy of the Lord, men meek, and not lovers of money, and truthful and proved; for they also render to you the service of prophets and teachers. Therefore do not despise them, for they are your honored ones, together with the prophets and teachers" (15:1–4, Roberts-Donaldson's translation). In contrast

Also absent from the Apostle's lists is the distinction of clergy and laity. Everybody has a special place in St. Paul's conception of the Church; everybody has gifts, and everybody has an office. Nowhere in the New Testament are Christians distinguished as *klērikos* or *laikos*. The casting of lots (*klēros*) is mentioned in the selection of St. Matthias a replacement apostle (Acts 1:17, 25), as is the people's selection of "the Seven" and their blessing by a laying-on of hands (Acts 6:3–7), but when the word *laos* is used to mean Christians in the New Testament (Acts 15:14, 2 Cor. 6:16, Titus 2:14, Heb., 4:9, 1 Peter 2:9–10), it includes all of the faithful, ordained and not ordained. The distinction of *klērikos* and *laikos* does not appear until the second or third century and only gradually takes hold.[170]

The only fundamental differences affecting the exercise of individual gifts in the New Testament are the difference between those who were or were not with Christ during His ministry (Acts 1:21–22) and the difference of male and female, Galatians 3:28 notwithstanding. The Apostle Paul does not deny that women receive the same gifts as men, but, as we have seen, he does limit what women may do with their gifts: They may not speak in the assembly, teach publicly, or exercise authority over men (1 Cor. 14:34–35, 1 Tim. 2:11–12). This effectively bars women from just one of the charismatic offices named by St. Paul: There are no women apostles.[171] There are women (and men) honored by the Church as "equal to the Apostles" (ἰσαπόστολος, *aequalis apostolis*) for having made disciples of nations, but there are

---

to the *Didache*'s emphasis on charismatic offices, St. Clement of Rome (+99) never mentions contemporary prophets or teachers in his epistle to the Corinthians (1 Clement) and speaks more often of elders generally than of bishops and deacons.

[170] In likening the order of the Temple to the order of the Church, St. Clement of Rome, in 1 Clement 40:5, mentions high priests, priests, Levites, and "laity" (*laikos*), but he does not directly correlate these to bishops, presbyters, deacons, and laymen (PG 1, 289). Nevertheless, this is often taken to be the first use of the term *laikos* for unordained Christians. Another Clement, Clement of Alexandria (AD 155–220), is the first to use the term *klērikos* in *Quis dives salvetur?* See Bradshaw (2002), 204, and Peter S.C. Pothan, "The Subjection of the Laity," *Religion and Society*, 55, 1–2 (March-June) 2010, 36–40.

[171] Both Priscilla and Aquila evangelized Apollos (Acts 18:26), and both were also honored by St. Paul as "my fellow-workers in Christ" (Rom. 16:3), and but only the husband, Aquila, was numbered about the Seventy Apostles. No women were.

no women who have been invested with the plenary responsibility and authority of an apostle to establish the Church among the nations.[172]

This still left women of the early Church with considerable freedom to prophesy, evangelize, teach, heal, shepherd, manage, minister, and serve without transgressing their apostolic limits. The New Testament gives us many examples of such women. Some of them may have received a special blessing for their work, maybe even an imposition of hands. Some like St. Phoebe may have been said at times to be *diakonoi* just as many men were said at times to be *diakonoi*, without meaning that they held a particular rank in the Church with particular responsibilities, authorities, or honors. Some women certainly were what we might now call "employees" or "staff members" of the Church—pious, dutiful, trustworthy women working full or part time at various tasks, either supporting themselves on account of their wealth or being supported by the Church as enrolled widows. Yet we must assume, as the Fathers all assumed, that in the apostolic era all apostolic ordinances governing relations between the sexes were respected and that nothing women were approved to do violated the natural and economic order of the sexes by elevating women over men in the order of the Church.

The Administrative Church

In addition to this original organic order, there is also an administrative order, which begins with the appointment of seven men to handle the daily distribution of aid to widows in need (Acts 6:1–6). This duty is called a διακονία in Acts 6:1, but it is also distinguished from the διακονία of the Apostles in Acts 6:4, the difference being that one is a prayerful "ministry of the word" while the other is a practical ministry of material needs. The practical ministry is immediately shown to be an additional duty that does not prevent the seven men from exercising their spiritual gifts. Stephen, the first of the seven, is a prophet who preaches boldly to unbelievers in public until he is martyred by them (Acts 6:8–15). Philip is soon called by an angel to leave Jerusalem and evangelize the countryside, starting with the Ethiopian eunuch (Acts 8:26–40). None of the seven are actually called

---

[172] Women honored by the Orthodox as equals-of-the-Apostles include Sts. Mary Magdalene, Photine the Samaritan, Thecla of Iconium, Empress Helen, Nina of Georgia, and Princess Olga of Russia.

"διάκονος" in the New Testament. Philip is instead identified as "the evangelist" and "one of the Seven" (Acts 21:8). Five of "the Seven" (Philip, Prochorus, Nicanor, Timon, and Parmenas) were later numbered among the Seventy Apostles.[173]

The familiar triad of bishop, presbyter, and deacon does not appear in writing until the early second century, in the epistles of St. Ignatius, but very early the duties of deacons are shown to be threefold: liturgical, pastoral, and administrative.[174] St. Ignatius himself testifies to their liturgical role, writing, "And those likewise who are deacons of the mysteries of Jesus Christ must please all men in all ways. For they are not deacons of meats and drinks but servants [ὑπηρέται] of the Church of God."[175] Later in the same century, St. Justin Martyr writes of deacons distributing Holy Communion to those in church and sending Communion to those absent.[176] St. Cyprian of Carthage likewise writes of deacons offering the Chalice and, in times of persecution, counseling martyrs in prison, hearing confessions, and pronouncing absolution with an imposition of hands.[177]

With these pastoral and liturgical duties came a degree of authority over the faithful. In his epistle to St. Polycarp, St. Ignatius writes that all the faithful are "subject to the bishop, the presbyters, the deacons."[178] The *Didascalia* tasks deacons with making sure people take

---

[173] Nicolaus, as the author of the Nicolaitan heresy, is not numbered among the Seventy Apostles.

[174] See K. Sutherland and P. Allen, "Many Gifts: One Form of Service," *New Blackfriars*, 58, 684 (May 1977) 215–216.

[175] Epistle to the Trallians, 2:3, PG 5, 676B–677A, J.B. Lightfoot's translation.

[176] In his *First Apology*, St. Justin writes: "And when the president has given thanks, and all the people have expressed their assent, those who are called by us deacons give to each of those present to partake of the bread and wine mixed with water over which the thanksgiving was pronounced, and to those who are absent they carry away a portion" (PG 6, 428B). Later, he says again that "to those who are absent a portion is sent by the deacons" (PG 6, 429C, Roberts-Donaldson's translation).

[177] See St. Cyprian's *On the Lapsed*, 25, PL 4, 485A–B; Epistle 10, PL 4, 254A–B; and Epistle 12, 259A–B.

[178] St. Ignatius, Epistle to Polycarp, 6:1, PG 5, 724B. In the fourth century, an unknown editor added similar words to St. Ignatius's epistle to the Ephesians: "Do ye, beloved, be careful to be subject to the bishop, and the presbyters and the deacons. For he that is subject to these is obedient to Christ, who has appointed them; but he that is disobedient to these is disobedient to Christ Jesus" (Epistle to the Ephesians, long recension, chapter 5, Roberts-Donaldson's

their proper places in church, "And let the deacon also see that no one whispers, or falls asleep, or laughs, or makes signs."[179] As we have seen, the *Apostolic Constitutions* gives deacons authority over subdeacons, readers, chanters, and deaconesses, calling them the deacon's ministers.[180] By the fourth century, the deacon had already assumed the commanding role in worship still in evidence today, telling the people when to pray, sing, stand, pay attention, bow their heads, send out the catechumens, and bar the doors. "If anyone misbehaves," says St. John Chrysostom, "call the deacon."[181]

The practical duties of deacons also involved the exercise of authority. The original *diakonia* delegated to the first deacons by the Apostles was not waiting tables in a dining hall; it was managing the material wealth of the congregation, a large part of which went to helping the needy. The "tables" mentioned in Acts 6:2 were for receiving donations and distributing aid. The same word (τράπεζα) is used in the Gospels for the tables of the moneychangers in the Temple. From this use, it came to mean "bank," for the same reason the benches (*banci*) used by Italian moneylenders (*banchieri*) gave their name to banks in the West (Italian *banca*, French *banque*, English *bank*). The Apostles wanted no part of this very worldly business, so they appointed others to decide who got what from the Church's treasury. St. John Chrysostom acknowledges the financial nature of this new office in his homily on Acts 6:

> But observe, I pray you, if there were need of seven men for this, great in proportion must have been the sums of money that flowed in, great in proportion also the number of widows. So then the prayers were not made in an off-hand way, but with much deliberate attention.[182]

In imitation of the Apostles, Pope Fabian of Rome (+250) divided the city into seven precincts, each administered by a deacon with a staff of

---

translation). On the spuriousness of the long recension, see Quasten, *Patrology*, 1.74.

[179] *Didascalia*, 12.
[180] *Apostolic Constitutions*, 8.3.28, ANF 7, 494.
[181] St. John Chrysostom, Homily 24 on Acts, PG 60, 190.
[182] St. John Chrysostom, Homily 14 on Acts, PG 60, 116, NPNF1 11, 91.

seven—one subdeacon and six acolytes. These seven deacons were responsible for recording the acts of martyrs, constructing catacombs, and caring for over 1,500 widows and indigents.[183] St. Lawrence was chief among them when he was martyred in 258.

The power of deacons was at times abused, of course, and in time provoked a reaction strictly limiting deacons' liturgical role and subordinating them not just to bishops but also to presbyters.[184] But the change of greatest import for deacons probably had less to do with the arrogance of deacons or the jealousy of presbyters than with the traditional attachment of deacons to bishops and the reluctance of bishops to give up parts of their thriving dioceses. Instead of ordaining another bishop to take over part of his diocese, a bishop would send presbyters to tend the flock on his behalf, and presbyters did not rate deacons.

As bishops relied more on presbyters to manage parishes in their stead, deacons became rarer, more temporary, and more limited in their duties. By the end of the fourth century, the diaconate had changed enough in some parts that St. John Chrysostom did not recognize "the Seven" of Acts 6 as either deacons or presbyters.[185] The Council *in Trullo* in 692 agreed and quoted him in its ruling that the Seven were not "deacons who served at the Mysteries"—they were just

---

[183] The *Liber Pontificalis* says of Fabian, "Hic regiones diuidit diaconibus et fecit VII subdiaconos qui VII notariis inminerent, ut gestas martyrum in integro fideliter colligerent, et multas fabricas per cymiteria fieri praecepit." See also Eusebius, *Ecclesiastical History*, 6.43.11, PG 20 621A, and Davies, 6–8.

[184] Complaints about deacons were commonplace, beginning with *The Shepherd of Hermas*, 26:2, which warns of "deacons that exercised their office ill, and plundered the livelihood of widows and orphans, and made gain for themselves from the ministrations which they had received to perform" (PG 2, 1002). In the fourth-century, an anonymous author penned a piece entitled *On the Boastfulness of Roman Deacons* (*De Jactantia Romanorum Levitarum*, PLS 3 3202). Two early canons (Canon 16 of Arles in 314 and Canon 18 of Nicaea in 325) prohibit deacons for presiding over the Eucharist. Many other early canons spell out the limits of the deacon's office and the reverence they owe presbyters. See Chryssavgis, 58–60, 86–89, and Edward Echlin, *The Deacon in the Church, Past and Future* (New York: Society of St. Paul, 1971), 54–71.

[185] On the Seven's ministry, Chrysostom reasons, "Was it that of Deacons? And yet this is not the case in the Churches. But is it to the Presbyters that the management belongs? And yet at present there was no bishop, but the Apostles only. Whence I think it clearly and manifestly follows, that neither Deacons nor Presbyters is their designation: but it was for this particular purpose that they were ordained" (Homily 14 on Acts, PG 60, 116, NPNF1 11, 90–91).

men charged with a particular nonsacramental duty, like today's epitrops, church wardens, and parish council members.[186] Even so, the Church's earliest tradition did regard them as deacons, and this tradition still survives and is now broadly accepted.[187]

The administrative role of deacons also survived the rise of the presbyters. Where there were still bishops, deacons continued to serve as their executive assistants, representing them at councils and at the imperial court and often succeeding them in office.[188] Deacons were still preaching in the fifth century and still distributing Holy Communion in the seventh.[189] Because of their closeness to their bishops, they were often the second most important man in the diocese, such that their ordinations as presbyters were sometimes seen as demotions.[190] In Constantinople, as at Rome, deacons were preferred for the highest offices of the patriarchal administration, serving as *oikonomos* (treasurer and property manager), *skeuophylax* (sacristan), *chartophylax* (librarian, archivist, and later patriarchal chancellor), *sakellarios*

---

[186] Canon 16, NPNF2 14, 373.

[187] St. Irenaeus of Lyon is the first to make the connection, identifying St. Stephen as "the first deacon elected by the apostles" (*Against Heresies*, 3.12.10, PG 7, 904B). St. Hippolytus of Rome, St. Cyprian of Carthage, and Eusebius of Caesarea also believed the Seven were deacons, and the Council of Neocaesarea in 315 followed Rome in limiting deacons to seven on the basis of Acts 6. See St. Hippolytus, *Refutation of All Heresies*, 7.24, ANF 5.115; St. Cyprian, Epistle 73, CC *Series Latina* III C, 539, ANF 5.381; Eusebius, *Ecclesiastical History*, 2.1; and Canon 15 of Neocaesarea, NPNF2 14, 86.

[188] St. Athanasius the Great was a deacon when he accompanied St. Alexander of Alexandria to Nicaea in 325, led the opposition to the Arius as Alexander's spokesman, and succeeded Alexander as patriarch in 328. Other examples include the deacon Dioscorus, who succeeded St. Cyril of Alexandria as patriarch in 444; the deacon Pelagius, who succeeded Pope Vigilius of Rome in 555; and the deacon Constantius, who succeeded Laurentius II as bishop of Milan in 573.

[189] Echlin, 76 and 81.

[190] In 453, Pope St. Leo the Great rebuked St. Anatolius of Constantinople "for degrading his archdeacon Aetius by making him a presbyter." See Echlin, 74. Pope St. Gregory the Great (+604) rebuked bishop Natalis of Salona for making his archdeacon, Honoratus, a presbyter against Honoratus's will to wrest control diocesan finances from him. Book 1, Epistles 19 and 20, PL 77, 464B–466A.

(treasurer, later supervisor of monasteries), and *synkellos* (personal aide and confidant of the patriarch and sometimes his successor).[191]

Needless to say, deaconesses could not share in this administrative ministry because they could not exercise authority over men. Even their authority over women was greatly limited by the fact that most women were under the authority of men—husbands, fathers, brothers, or uncles, besides bishops, presbyters, and deacons. For that reason, if for no other, the appointment of female presidents or *presbytides* was forbidden, as any such appointment would have tended to establish a separate chain of command for women at odds with existing legal and social arrangements as well as the natural and ecclesiastical order.

The Hierarchic Church

If in the organic Church there is an order of precedence, based on diversities of gifts, and in the administrative Church there is an order of authority, based on delegated responsibility, there is also in the hierarchic Church an order of illumination, based on the priestly activity of the more illumined imparting illumination to the less illumined. It begins with Christ Himself enlightening the Apostles and commissioning them to enlighten others.

In time, this priestly activity came to dominate the Church's understanding of holy orders. The ranks of the Church came to be defined by their distinct sacramental roles, with each rank licensed to do everything permitted to lower ranks, but with lower ranks forbidden to do things set aside for higher ranks. Bishops and priests came to be called "priests" (ἱερεύς in Greek, *sacerdos* in Latin) for their essential participation in the celebration of the Sacraments. The new terminology stressed their role as mediators between God and the people over their role as overseers, elders, and presidents of the assembly. This happened first in the West in the works of Tertullian, St. Cyprian of Carthage, and the *Apostolic Tradition* of St. Hippolytus. Whether the change represented a new development or merely a new expression of traditional relationship is a point of debate, as are the reasons for the

---

[191] B. David Kennedy, "Diaconate in the Ukrainian Catholic Church," *Chrysostom*, 7, No. 1 (Spring, 1985), 11.

change.[192] Nevertheless, the change did occur, coinciding with the increasingly common distinction of *klērikos* and *laikos*, the growth of monasticism and the cult of virginity, and the influence (through Origen and Evagrius Ponticus) of Platonism, with its characteristic contrast of the gnostic few against the agnostic many, all of which combined to create the sense that among Christians there were classes of holiness reflected in the ranks of the Church.

Such thinking received its fullest development in the "hierarchy" of the sixth-century writer known today as Pseudo-Dionysius or Dionysius the Areopagite.[193] Building on the Neoplatonism of Proclus, Dionysius defined his neologism ἱεραρχία as a "holy order and knowledge and activity" (τάξις ἱερά καὶ ἐπιστήμη καὶ ἐνέργεια) uplifting rational beings toward an imitation of God, as much as they are able, by passing on illumination from higher ranks to lower ranks.[194] "Each rank around God conforms more to him than the one farther away," he writes.[195] It is therefore difficult if not impossible to avoid the impression that Dionysius's Church is a spiritual meritocracy based on degrees of holiness, there being no other way for a true hierarchy to

---

[192] See Bradshaw (2002), 201–205. He writes: "Some conservative scholars would understand this to be merely the gradual unfolding of a reality which was already present in the priesthood of Christ and shared from the outset by bishops and presbyters, who acted in the place of Christ (*vice Christi*), even though Cyprian was the first to articulate this idea explicitly (Epistle 63.14, PL 4, 386A). Others would understand it to be a genuinely new development at the end of the second century, marking the inception of a major change in the relationship between the people and their ministers within the Church: bishops and presbyters would eventually cease to be seen as the presiders within a priestly people, and become instead a priesthood acting on behalf of 'the laity'—a term already used in this sense in *1 Clement* 40.5. Although thereafter liturgical texts themselves might still carry the more ancient image of the common priesthood in which all Christians participated, both theological discourse and ecclesiastical practice instead viewed ordination rather than baptism as the decisive point of entry into the priestly life."
[193] I am persuaded by Ernesto Sergio Mainoldi that Pseudo-Dionysius was a student of Proclus and convert from Neoplatonism named Hegias writing in the early sixth century in support of Justinian's political, ecclesiastical, and theological program. See Mainoldi's "Why Dionysius the Areopagite? The Invention of the First Father." In *Studia Patristica Vol. XCVI*, edited by Markus Vinzent, 425–40. Leuven: Peeters, 2017.
[194] Pseudo-Dionysius, *Celestial Hierarchy* 3.1, PG 3, 164D.
[195] Pseudo-Dionysius, *Letter 8 to Demophilus*, PG 3, 1092B, Liubheid's translation.

function.[196] It consists of three clerical ranks (*hierarchēs, hiereus,* and *leitourgos*) and three lay ranks: those being perfected ("the most exalted order" of monks), those being illumined ("the order of the sacred people"), and those being purified (penitents and catechumens).[197] Clergy are distinguished from laity by their priestly responsibility for purifying, illumining, and perfecting others.[198] Throughout his works, Dionysius stresses the inequality of persons, repeatedly disparaging the *hoi polloi* while rhapsodizing on the lordliness of the "godlike hierarch" (*theoeidēs hierarchēs*) who alone contemplates awesome mysteries while the laity content themselves with symbols.[199] Our Lord's many warnings that in the Kingdom the greatest shall be the humblest (Matt. 18:3) and that "many that are first shall be last, and the last shall be first" are never mentioned by Dionysius in any of his works.[200] Neither is the Apostle Paul's exhortation, "in lowliness of mind let each esteem others better than themselves." (Phil. 2:3)

The narrowness of Dionysius's vision, confined as it is to the priestly illumination of lessers by greaters, leaves him with little to say about relations between equals and nothing at all to say about natural

---

[196] Andrew Louth writes, "Though, clearly, the priestly orders derive their authority from their priestly consecration, Denys often speaks as if they derive their authority from their intrinsic, moral and intellectual qualities. He comes very close to suggesting that the efficacy of a priest's ministrations depend upon his own holiness and purity: he is very far from any Augustinian notion of the validity of orders which guarantees the efficacy of the ministry of the unworthy priest." Louth, *Denys the Areopagite* (Wilton, Conn.: Morehouse-Barlow, 1989), 65–66. Balthasar takes a similar view, likening Dionysius's position to that of Tertullian and the Donatists sans their "sectarian zeal." Balthasar, *The Glory of God: A Theological Aesthetic,* Vol. 2 (Edinburgh: T&T Clark, 1984), 175.

[197] Pseudo-Dionysius, *Ecclesiastical Hierarchy* 6, PG 3, 532A–533A, in Luibheid, 243–245.

[198] Pseudo-Dionysius, *Ecclesiastical Hierarchy* 6, PG 3, 533C.

[199] Of the hierarch, Dionysius writes: "When he has received and distributed the supremely Divine Communion, he terminates with a holy thanksgiving; whilst the multitude have merely glanced at the Divine symbols alone, he is ever conducted by the Divine Spirit, as becomes a Hierarch, in the purity of a Godlike condition, to the holy sources of the things performed, in blessed and intelligible visions." Pseudo-Dionysius, *Ecclesiastical Hierarchy* 3, PG 3, 428A, Parker's translation. Cf. Luibheid, 211.

[200] Matt. 19:30, cf. Matt. 20:16, Mark 9:35, Mark 10:31, Mark 10:42–45, Luke 13:30, Luke 22:24–26.

family relations or male/female relations.[201] This gender neutrality might seem to leave open the possibility of women participating in the ecclesiastical hierarchy in the rank of *leitourgos*, if not also in the ranks of *hiereus* and *hierarchēs*—except that Holy Scripture and Apostolic Tradition are not silent on that subject, and when what they say is added to a strictly hierarchical understanding of holy orders, no room is left for women clerics. This is the view expressed above by Matthew Blastares in his dismissal of Theodore Balsamon's opinion that menstruation was the reason for excluding women from the altar. Blastares's words are worth re-quoting:

> However, it does not appear plausible to me that a woman became a deacon of the Sacred and Bloodless Sacrifice, as there is no sound reason why women, who are not permitted to teach in public, should be raised to the rank of the diaconate, whose work is to purify orally those unbelievers that come forward for baptism.[202]

Here Blastares connects the Apostle's prohibition on women teaching publicly with Dionysius's peculiar identification of the deacon's purpose of purification to conclude that women cannot be deacons. This is evidence not only of Dionysius's influence on Byzantine thinking but also of the impact of that influence on the order of deaconess. For Blastares, the diaconate was a rank in the ecclesiastical hierarchy and a rank women could not fill because of the limits imposed on them by the Apostles out of respect for the natural and economic order of male and female. It therefore made no sense to him for women to be made "deacons."

We have no reason to believe that Blastares was alone in this opinion. Quite the contrary: We have every reason to believe that others

---

[201] Of relations between godlike equals, Dionysius merely says a few times in passing that they keep company with each other in a "mutually regarding union" (*koinōnikēn allēlouchian*). See Pseudo-Dionysius, *Divine Names* 4, PG 3, 709D, cf. 708A, 713B.

[202] Matthew Blastares, *Syntagma, littera Gamma*, PG 144, 1173D, translated by Viscuso, 111: "Γυναῖκα δὲ τῆς ἱερᾶς καὶ ἀναιμάκτου γίνεσθαι θυσίας διάκονον, οὔ μοι δοκεῖ τὸ πιθανὸν ἔχειν· ὡς ἔστιν οὐ λόγον σῶζον, τὰς μὴ συγχωρουμένας δημοσίᾳ διδάσκειν, εἰς διακόνου βαθμὸν ἀνέναι, οἷς ἔργον τὸ διὰ λόγου καθαίρειν τοὺς προσιόντας τῶν ἀπίστων ἐπὶ τὸ βάπτισμα."

before and after him thought the same way. With no change in the Church's understanding of the natural and economic order, but with a change instead from an organic understanding of the Church to a more administrative and hierarchical understanding, ordaining women as "deacons" or "deaconesses" made less and less sense to many Byzantines, especially many clergymen. Because of the order's supposedly apostolic institution, they could not vocally oppose the order without seeming impious, but they could and did discourage it by severely limiting and then eventually abandoning it, and when it was gone, they gave reasons for it only to stay gone.

CONCLUSION

A Unified Theory of the Female Diaconate

Having summarized what is known of deaconesses, and having enlarged the context in which to evaluate what is known of deaconesses to include Church teaching on male and female as well as changes in the church order, we can now offer a clearer, fuller, more plausible, and more consistent theory of the origin, evolution, decline, and disappearance of the female diaconate.

In the apostolic Church, both men and women exercised their spiritual gifts and used their worldly resources to advance the Gospel through various forms of trusted service or *diakonia*. Some such people were especially helpful and effective, becoming what we today might call the "go-to person" for particular services. Some were also especially pious, forgoing marriage to dedicate themselves solely to Christian service, with or without formal recognition of their status. St. Phoebe of Cenchrea was such a person—faithful, able, trustworthy, and of course respectful of the rules of behavior governing the assembly, including the prohibitions on women speaking publicly and exercising authority over men.

Following the example of Christ, leadership of the Church remained in the hands of men—first the Apostles and then the elders, who came to be sorted into two and then three ranks: bishops, presbyters, and deacons. The least of these was labeled with a very common Greek word, used for virtually any service provided by any trusted person, from Christ on down, but also used increasingly to mean a bishop's executive assistant. The dual use of this word by Greek speakers caused some later Christians to assume greater similarity between the male "deacons" they knew personally and the female "deacon" they read about in Romans 16:1. It was then only a matter of time before someone somewhere proposed making women "deacons" to handle some deacon-like duty, which the pseudonymous author of the *Didascalia Apostolorum* did in Syria in the early third century.

Even with the supposed mention of women deacons in the New Testament and the pretended recommendation of the Apostles in the *Didascalia Apostolorum*, the order of deaconess was slow to catch on. Actual deaconesses are first heard to exist among the Paulianist heretics of Syria in the early fourth century. Decades later Western Christians still had never heard of them except among heretics. Their Latin Bibles never identified Phoebe as a "deacon." Their councils in Gaul repeatedly condemned the novelty of deaconesses, and though the fashion did eventually catch on in Italy and Sicily under Byzantine influence, deaconesses remained virtually unknown throughout the rest of the West, not to mention Egypt.

The order did take hold in the empire's major Eastern cities, as a way to consecrate women to monastic service, as a reward for wealthy patronesses, and as a consolation for the wives of men made bishops. At some point, an essentially monastic rite of ordination was composed resembling that of deacons to enhance the appearance of the honor, which actually involved quite little in terms of responsibilities and prerogatives. Compared to deacons, deaconesses are much less in evidence in ancient texts and inscriptions. Church Fathers have little to say about the order when not trying to explain Romans 16:1 or 1 Timothy 3:11. Whereas deacons appear in almost every collection of ecclesiastical canons, deaconesses rarely do. Thirty of the 85 Apostolic Canons mention deacons; not one mentions deaconesses.

Of their traditional duty—assisting in the baptism of women—we hear little beyond occasional mentions of it as their traditional duty, when a reason for the order needed mentioning. Similarly, when the order needed a reason for having ceased to exist, infant baptism was sometimes said to have eliminated the need for it. But we never actually hear of deaconesses assisting in baptism, and it is impossible to gauge how active deaconesses were in this duty. As much of the ancient Church recognized, deaconesses were never really needed to assist in baptism; any nun or pious laywoman could complete the anointing of naked women, or the priest could say his prayers and do his best.

Despite the leading role of deaconesses in early monastic communities, the Church outside Syria did not make ordination as a deaconess a requirement for the office of abbess and instead adopted a special blessing for abbesses. We might speculate on the reasons: The title of deacon was strongly associated with the role of assisting rather than presiding; the traditional duties of deaconesses did not include presiding over groups of women; all ordinations were for sacramental service, but an abbess's duties were administrative and pastoral and not sacramental; adding sacramental service to the office of abbess while also adding the duty of presiding to the rank of deaconess would have exalted deaconesses against presbyters and deacons, making them a little more than deacons and a little less than priests, which would have challenged both the gender order and the church order.

The Church did not experience a shift away from a more egalitarian regard for gender. On the contrary, it was challenged within and without to become more sexually egalitarian. It contended against heretical sects that featured women prominently in their leadership and worship. It also contended at times against assertive women rulers and aristocrats. Sometimes such women championed the orthodox cause; sometimes they did not. From the fifth century onward, the Church experienced a dramatic feminization of popular piety with the addition of several new feasts celebrating the Theotokos. Today, of course, we can appreciate the balance this brought to our understanding of God and man, but it could have been seen long ago as a potential threat to the natural order. When told by Nestorius that "only priests may walk here," the Empress Pulcheria is said to have replied, "Why? Have I not given birth to God?"[203] This incident raises the possibility that Nestorius's objection to the title *Theotokos* was in part a reaction to nascent feminism inspired by the veneration of the Virgin, with whom the virgin empress identified. The decline of the deaconess did, in fact, coincide with the rise of the Theotokos. The latter may have contributed to the former, not by changing the gender order but by challenging it, perhaps obliging Church Fathers to exercise more care in maintaining

---

[203] On the encounter between St. Pulcheria and Nestorius, see Nicholas P. Constas, "Weaving the Body of God," *Journal of Early Christian Studies* 3 (1995) 173–174, and Kenneth G. Holum, *Theodosian Empresses: Women and Imperial Dominion in Late Antiquity* (Berkeley: University of California Press, 1982), 152–155.

proper limits. The Byzantine rite of ordination may also have challenged the gender order, bringing women too close to the altar for the clergy's comfort and giving deaconesses a false sense of their own importance. If ordaining a deaconess meant giving her an orar and handing her the Chalice, more bishops may have opted against ordination.

Greatly limited by general restrictions on women and specific restrictions on deaconesses, and serving no essential purpose, the order withered after peaking in the fifth or sixth century, surviving mainly in Constantinople as a distinctive adornment of the Great Church and the imperial court. Known for their singing, they were in time joined in singing by non-ordained nuns, who also came to be called deaconesses. This combined choir survived the end of the order of deaconesses, consisting then solely of non-ordained nuns perhaps with the new name of "Myrrhbearers," which Anthony of Novgorod mentions.

We can only wonder whether the order would have evolved differently and lasted longer if it had not shared the name of "deacon." The name was both a blessing and a curse for the order, adding to the prestige of being a deaconess but also raising questions about the standing of deaconesses vis-à-vis other clergy. Treating deaconesses like deacons exalted them above subdeacons, readers, chanters, and all laymen, which brought them into conflict with the Church's fundamental beliefs about the man and the woman. This accounts for both the outright resistance to female "deacons" in the West and the waning enthusiasm for female "deacons" in the East, which led ultimately to their disappearance.

The same theory also accounts for the current controversy over applying the name once again to women. One side covets the title of "deacon," preferring it over "deaconess," because it no longer believes in the subjection of the woman and wants to see women treated equally with men, in the Church as in the world. The other side hasn't given up on the subjection of the woman and fears that if it gives up on women deacons it will be hard pressed to invent a reason not to also give up on women priests and women bishops. There is only one reason found in the Fathers.

"Tradition or History?"

Remarks by Protodeacon Brian Patrick Mitchell
at the St. Phoebe Center Conference on
"Renewing the Male and Female Diaconate"
Irvine, California
October 7, 2017

Thank you, Helen [Theodoropoulos], for the introduction, and thanks also to AnnMarie Mecera and everyone else at the St. Phoebe Center for the opportunity to speak here today, especially Marilyn Rouvelas, who made the introduction, and Fr. Peter Danilchick, who suggested my name when the need appeared.

I'm, of course, representing myself here today and no one else—not my jurisdiction and not my bishop—so the opinions I express today are mine and mine alone.

The first point I want to make is that, for all of the research done on deaconesses in recent decades, we still know very little about them. There are two main reasons for that: One is that their role was always very limited, so there's just not much said about them in ancient texts, compared to what's said about bishops, priests, or deacons. Another reason is that their presence was also always very limited: There weren't many of them anywhere except in some of the larger cities of the eastern empire like Constantinople. In many places, there weren't any at all, and for a long time, there weren't any anywhere in the Orthodox Church.

That's something to keep in mind when we think about the place of deaconesses in Orthodox tradition: The whole Church has never had a tradition of having deaconesses, but the whole Church has had a tradition of *not* having them—even after having had them, in some places.

The question is, why? There are two reasons, both rather obvious: One is infant baptism, which explains why churches that had deaconesses stopped having them. But it doesn't explain why other churches never had them. The obvious answer to that question is that the office of deaconess was inherently problematic, because it appeared to elevate women over men in the hierarchy of the Church, contrary to Christian conceptions about both the natural order and the divine economy.

This explains not only why some churches never had deaconesses, but also (a) why deaconesses were so few in numbers in the churches that had them, (b) why their duties were always greatly limited, (c) why they eventually disappeared from churches that had them, and (d) why they were not revived for so many centuries thereafter.

Now, one could still argue that the fact that great churches of the East did have deaconesses, and the fact that great saints of those churches like St. John Chrysostom did seem to have no problem with them, prove that early Christians were more accepting of women in leadership roles than later Christians came to be.

The problem with that argument—and it's an especially big problem for the Orthodox—is that it takes a fundamentally Protestant approach to Christian tradition. It asks us to believe that the first Christians were really quite progressive in their thinking, but, along the way, things went terribly wrong, and we're only now getting back to real Christianity.

Daphne Hampson, a feminist critic of Christian feminism, calls this the "golden thread" approach to Christian tradition: You pick a favorite part of tradition and seize on it as the key to everything. For Martin Luther, it was "justification by faith." For Christian feminists, it's "neither male nor female." Everything in line with "neither male nor female"—deaconesses, empresses, female saints—is held up as part of the golden thread of true faith, and whatever is not in line is dismissed as historical clutter. It's an approach that pits scripture against scripture and tradition against tradition, privileging supposedly egalitarian scriptures and traditions over patriarchal scriptures and traditions, which are blamed on alien influence.

Of course, once you take that approach, it's Katy-bar-the-door, because everything but the golden thread is expendable. We've seen where that approach has gotten Protestants generally, and we've seen where it has gotten Protestant feminists. Not content with female deacons, they went on to demand female priests and female bishops—and they got gay priests and gay bishops, and now transgenders, because, of course, if gender doesn't matter, then gender doesn't matter. That's what you get when you understand "neither male nor female" absolutely.

A saner, more Orthodox, more plainly Christian approach would be to seek not conflict but consistency in scripture and not corruption but continuity in tradition. Not that nothing ever changes in the Church. There will always be adjustments to historical circumstances, as well as mistakes made and lessons learned. But the principles will remain the same at all times.

Now, I'm going to state and explain a principle, and then I'm going to briefly explain the Church's experience with deaconesses according to that principle. The principle is: "The head of the woman is the man, and the head of the man is Christ, and the head of Christ is God."

That's 1 Corinthians 11:3. I could talk at length about what it means. (It's the subject of my dissertation.) But the key thing to know about this verse is that it's not about inequality. Just the opposite: It's about equality. That's how Theodoret of Cyrus understood this verse. In fact, he used the verse to argue that the Son is equal to the Father because the Father is the source of the Son, and Greek speakers much more often used the word *kephalē* ["head"] to mean "source" than to mean "ruling power." In fact, in the Septuagint, the word *kephalē* is used interchangeably with the word *archē* to translate the Hebrew word *rosh*, meaning "head" or "beginning," as in *Rosh Hashanah*, the beginning of the new year. We have a similar usage in English of the word *headwater*, meaning the source of a river.

So we have an equality based on *sourceness*, and what this means for God and Christ, and for the man and the woman, is that they relate to each other through self-giving by the source and thanksgiving by the other. In the Gospels, between the Father and the Son, all of the giving is done by the Father and all the thanking is done by the Son. Not once is the Father said to thank the Son, and not once is the Son said to give anything to the Father except thanks.

Now, between the Father and the Son, this relationship of self-giving and thanksgiving involves no subjection and no obedience as we think of it. That's because of the one divine will, shared by the Father and the Son, who are in perfect agreement about everything. It's only

73

the Son's human will that must be brought under subjection and made obedient to the divine will.

But among mere humans since the Fall, there is no unity of will, and the only way we can be brought back into true unity—the only way "that they may be one as we are one"—is for one to submit to the other. And this is thus decreed by God for our own good, as St. John Chrysostom says when preaching on 1 Corinthians:

> And from the beginning He made one sovereignty only, setting the man over the woman. But after our race ran headlong into extreme disorder, He appointed other sovereignties also, those of Masters, and those of Governors, and this too for love's sake. [Homily 34 on 1 Cor.]

This is not what many Westerners believe today. Whether they know it or not, they are followers of Rousseau and Marx and others who despised humility and obedience and condemned subjection itself as tyranny, teaching people to take offense at being cast in the role of Christ—as the one to obey, the one to submit.

Truly, if Rousseau and Marx are our apostles, then we are in the wrong religion, because the Church of Christ has always taught humble acceptance of both our subjection to others and our *archic* and *eucharistic* responsibilities to others.

Now, what does this mean for deaconesses?

In the apostolic Church, as still today, both men and women used their spiritual gifts and worldly resources to advance the Gospel through various forms of trusted service or *diakonia*. Some such people were especially helpful and effective, becoming what we today might call the "go-to person" for particular services. Some were also especially pious, forgoing marriage to dedicate themselves solely to Christian service, with or without formal recognition of their status. St. Phoebe was such a person—faithful, able, trustworthy, and of course respectful of all of the rules of behavior governing the assembly, including the prohibitions on women speaking publicly and exercising authority over men.

In the East, but not in the West, the use of the word *diakonos* to describe such women, as St. Paul does in Romans 16:1, led eventually to the creation of a clerical order of female "deacons," which we see for the first time with certainty in the third-century, in the *Didascalia Apostolorum*, probably from Syria.

This new order was slow to catch on. In the fourth century, Western Christians were surprised to learn that there were deaconesses in the East, and they resisted their appearance in the West. Even in the East, deaconesses remained rather rare. Already in the sixth century, we hear it said by Severus of Antioch that the order was largely honorary, there being little real need for them.

At some point, a rite of ordination was composed resembling that of deacons. This rite appears in only about a dozen Byzantine euchologies, out of an estimated 2,000 still in existence. The rite certainly makes deaconesses look a lot like deacons, but it may actually have contributed to the order's demise by bringing women too close to the altar for the clergy's comfort. If ordaining a deaconess meant giving her an orar and handing her the Chalice, more and more bishops may have opted against ordaining them.

That's certainly what more and more bishops did, for whatever reason. They couldn't easily argue against the order of deaconesses because of the presumption in the East that the order was apostolic, but they weren't required to ordain any, and so they didn't.

All along, it's clear that deacons and deaconesses were never really the same order. They always existed on a very different basis on account of the fundamental difference of male and female. One order was ecumenical; the other order was regional. One was accepted everywhere without question; the other was resisted throughout much of the Church and eventually abandoned by the whole Church.

We can only wonder whether the order of deaconess would have evolved differently and lasted longer if it had not shared the name of "deacon." The name was both a blessing and a curse for the order, adding to the prestige of being a deaconess but also raising questions about the standing of deaconesses vis-à-vis other clergy. Treating deaconesses like deacons exalted them above subdeacons, readers, chanters, and all laymen, which brought them into conflict with the Church's fundamental beliefs about the man and the woman. This accounts for both the outright resistance to deaconesses in the West and the waning enthusiasm for deaconesses in the East.

This also explains the current controversy over applying the name once again to women. One side covets the title of "deacon," preferring it to the title of "deaconess," because it no longer believes in the subjection of women and wants to see women treated equally with men, in the Church as in the world. The other side hasn't given up on the natural order or the divine economy and knows that if it gives up on women deacons it will be hard pressed to invent a reason not to also give up on women priests and women bishops.

Remember: We've already seen where this leads and won't be fooled by assurances that things won't go too far. Already, from what I'm told, the new deaconesses in the Congo are performing the duties of readers—duties never associated with deaconesses in the ancient Church. And if deaconesses can read the Epistle, why can't they chant petitions? That's what more people will think, especially a generation from now, when the principle of male headship has been visibly repudiated by the admission of women to the ranks of the clergy.

The world now offers women more opportunities than ever before, and we've heard today moving testimony on the great things women can do to live a fuller life in Christ. But making them "deacons" will divide the Church. That last thing the Church needs today is another reason for division, and the last thing each of us needs today is another excuse not to practice the humility that's required of us.

We are called to be divine, and in divinity there is neither tyranny nor rebellion. There is only truth, love, and humble acceptance of the gifts we are offered, including the gift of our creation as male or female and the gift of our adoption as joint-heirs in Christ. That's the only way we can be saved. That's the only way men and women can be equal as the Father and the Son are equal and one as they are one, in the name of the Father and of the Son and of the Holy Spirit.

APPENDIX B:

"A Public Statement on Orthodox Deaconesses by Concerned Clergy and Laity"[204]
January 15, 2018

The Patriarchate of Alexandria's appointment of six "deaconesses" in the Congo in February 2017 has prompted calls in some corners for other local churches to follow suit. In particular, a group of Orthodox liturgical scholars has issued an open statement of support for Alexandria, declaring that the "restoration of the female diaconate is such that neither doctrinal issues nor authoritative precedents are at stake."[205]

We, the undersigned clergy and laity, beg to differ and are writing now with three purposes: to question what was accomplished in the Congo, to clarify the historical record on the place of deaconesses in Orthodox tradition, and to point out the serious doctrinal issues raised by the appointment of deaconesses.

First, as to what was accomplished in the Congo, we note that the Patriarch of Alexandria did not use the Byzantine rite of ordination for deaconesses.[206] He laid hands [*cheirothetisa*] on one woman making her "Deaconess of the Mission" and then prayed over five other women

---

[204] This statement, signed by 57 Orthodox clergymen and lay leaders and with an accompanying press release, was published originally by the American Orthodox Institute, where it may still be found at https://www.aoiusa.org/a-public-statement-on-orthodox-deaconesses-by-concerned-clergy-and-laity-2/. The statement has since garnered nearly 300 additional signatories. The footnotes that follow were all in the statement when published.

[205] Evangelos Theodorou, et al., "Orthodox Liturgists Issued a Statement of Support for the Revival of the Order of Deaconess by the Patriarchate of Alexandria," *Panorthodox Synod*, https://panorthodoxcemes.blogspot.ca/2017/10/orthodox-liturgists-issued-statement-of.html?m=1, Oct. 24, 2017.

[206] See "Το Πατριαρχείο Αλεξανδρείας για Διακόνισσες και Αγία Σύνοδο," Romfea, http://www.romfea.gr/epikairotita-xronika/11485-to-patriarxeio-alejandreias-gia-diakonisses-kai-agia-sunodo, Nov. 16, 2016; and, "Στην Αφρική εόρτασε τα ονομαστήρια του ο Πατριάρχης Θεόδωρος," Romfea, http://www.romfea.gr/patriarxeia-ts/patriarxeio-alexandreias/13147-stin-afriki-eortase-ta-onomastiria-tou-o-patriarxis-theodoros-foto, Feb. 18, 2017.

using a "prayer for one entering ecclesiastical ministry," a generic blessing in the Greek-language *archieratikon* for a layman starting church work. He did not bestow an orarion upon any of the women yet had the five women assist in washing his hands, as subdeacons would. All this was done not during the Divine Liturgy, as with an ordination, but at its end. These facts, plus anecdotal reports from Africa that these new deaconesses have been assigned the duties of readers, call into question the claim that what happened in the Congo was truly a "restoration of the female diaconate," for their manner of making and assigned duties bear only partial resemblance to those of ancient deaconesses.

Second, what can be said with certainty about the historical presence, role, and status of deaconesses in the Orthodox Church is that setting apart women as deaconesses was just one of several ways the early Church sought to protect the modesty of women by entrusting certain women with certain duties such as assisting in baptizing and anointing adult women and visiting women in their homes where and when men were not permitted, strictly within the limits specified for women by the Holy Apostles in Holy Scripture. The duties and status of deaconesses varied with time and place, as did the way deaconesses were appointed. The same duties were also assigned to widows, laywomen, male clergy, or nuns, so the need for deaconesses did not exist universally. Much of the ancient Church never had deaconesses. Outside Syria, Anatolia, Greece, and Palestine, deaconesses were rare to nonexistent.[207]

Deaconesses were also not without controversy. Several local councils prohibited their appointment (Nîmes in 396; Orange in 441; Epaone in 517; Orleans in 533), and many texts testify to the concern of Church Fathers to minimize their role, sometimes in favor of widows. The order appears to have peaked in the fifth or sixth century,

---

[207] For the most in-depth study of the subject, see Aimé Georges Martimort, *Deaconesses: An Historical Study*, trans. K.D. Whitehead (San Francisco: Ignatius Press, 1986). For a thorough study of Orthodox deaconesses before their disappearance, see Brian Patrick Mitchell, "The Disappearing Deaconess: How the Hierarchical Ordering of the Church Doomed the Female Diaconate," http://www.brianpatrickmitchell.com/wp-content/uploads/2012/09/Disappearing-Deaconess-2017-03-10.pdf. [EDITOR'S NOTE: "The Disappearing Deaconess" is now included in this volume and no longer available at brianpatrickmitchell.com.]

surviving mainly in major eastern cities as an honorary office for pious noblewomen, the wives of men made bishops, and the heads of female monastic communities. The twelfth-century canonist Theodore Balsamon wrote that the "deaconesses" in Constantinople in his day were not true deaconesses. A century later, St. Athanasius, Patriarch of Constantinople, ordered that no new deaconesses were to be made. Scattered proposals and attempts to appoint deaconesses again in the nineteenth and twentieth centuries did not receive enough support to cause a lasting revival of the order. Even now, other autocephalous Orthodox Churches have not rushed to follow the example of Alexandria.

Third, some blame resistance to deaconesses on a worldly, purely cultural prejudice against women, but that accusation treats the Church herself unfairly, even contemptuously, by ignoring legitimate prudential objections to the making of deaconesses motivated by genuine concern for the preservation of truly Christian and plainly Apostolic respect for the distinction of male and female, to which our post-Christian world is increasingly hostile.

The liturgists' statement itself gives cause for such concern. Its argument for "reviving" the order of deaconess is not based on the needs of the women to be served by deaconesses—needs that somehow require ordination, needs that nuns, laywomen, laymen, or male clergy are not already meeting. Rather, the statement's argument is based on the supposed need of women to be deaconesses. Making them deaconesses would be a "positive response" to the "contemporary world," an "opportunity for qualified women to offer in our era their unique and special gifts," and a "special way" to emphasize the "dignity of women and give recognition to her [sic] contribution to the work of the Church."[208] Such justifications denigrate the vocation of Orthodox laity, implying that only clerics serve the Church in meaningful ways, contrary to Orthodox belief that all Orthodox Christians receive the gifts of the Holy Spirit and a personal calling to serve the Church at Holy Chrismation.

---

[208] The "positive response" and "special way" are from the report of the Inter-Orthodox Symposium in Rhodes in 1988 titled, "The Place of the Woman in the Orthodox Church and the Question of the Ordination of Women" (Istanbul: The Ecumenical Patriarchate, 1988), which the liturgists quote approvingly.

The liturgists' statement also makes clear that they do not intend a true "restoration" of the ancient order of deaconesses; their aim is a new order of clergywomen authorized to do things never done by Orthodox deaconesses and in some cases explicitly forbidden by Apostolic ordinance and Church canons. They would have women preach, which the Apostles and Fathers never allowed in church. They leave open the question of other liturgical duties, admitting no limitation that bishops must respect. They question which "qualities and qualifications" truly matter, doubting whether deaconesses must be mature and unmarried, despite the ancient rule, most forcefully insisted upon in the sixth century by St. Justinian as emperor, that deaconesses be at least middle-aged and remain celibate as deaconesses.[209]

The liturgists' most ominous assertion is their subtle note, in anticipation of popular opposition, that "adequate preparation and education" are needed not of the women to be appointed deaconesses but "of the people who will be called upon to receive, honor, and respect the deaconesses assigned to their parishes." Clearly, they foresee the need to force clergy and laity to accept deaconesses, which is hardly trusting of the Holy Spirit or respectful of the Orthodox Church's traditional regard for episcopal authority.

In sum, the statement's emphasis on gratifying women, disregarding tradition, and resorting to force gives evidence of a feminist perspective and approach consistent with the faithless western world but not with the Orthodox Church. More evidence of the liturgists' perspective is available elsewhere. For example, two of the liturgists have called for the removal of Ephesians 5 from the Rite of Crowning on the grounds that it is inconsistent with modern thinking and therefore likely to be misunderstood. They suggest a different epistle or perhaps a sanitized version of Ephesians 5 without verse 33 ("Nevertheless let

---

[209] The minimum age for deaconesses changed several times over the years: The emperor St. Theodosius the Great set it at 60 in 390, the age the Apostle Paul set for enrolled widows in 1 Timothy 5:9, which St. Theodosius's legislation mentioned. Canon 15 of Chalcedon lowered it to 40 in 451. St. Justinian's Novella 6 raised it to 50 in 535, making an exception for women living in hermitages and having no contact with men. His Novella 123 lowered it to 40 again in 546, which Canon 14 of III Constantinople (*in Trullo*) confirmed in 692.

every one of you in particular so love his wife even as himself; and the wife see that she reverence [*phobētai*, fear] her husband.").[210]

Given this state of faith, we believe the appointment of deaconesses in any form in the present era is likely to divide the Church and distress the faithful by challenging the Church's basic understanding of human nature. God has made every one of us either male or female and ordained that we live accordingly as either a man or a woman. He has also provided us with many authoritative precepts distinguishing men and women, in the Law, in the Holy Apostles, in the canons of the Church, and in the literature of our Holy Fathers, in passages too numerous to cite. But if laws and canons and precepts are not enough to turn us to repentance, God has given us two distinct models of perfected humanity, one male and one female: Jesus Christ, the Incarnate Word of God, and His Most Pure Mother, the Theotokos, whose icons stand always before us in worship as reminders of what we are meant to be as men and women.

Yet there are advocates of deaconesses who wish to see women treated the same as men in the Church as in the world and who therefore use the rite of "ordination" (*cheirotonia*) of deaconesses in a handful of Byzantine service books to argue that deaconesses were once "major clergy." These advocates covet the rank, honor, and authority of the clergy. Some would have deaconesses be just like deacons, only female. They would up-end the natural and economical order of male and female to raise women over men in the hierarchy of the Church. They would "ordain" women who are young, married, and with children, and they would give them a vocal role in worship and all the authority a deacon might exercise over men as well as women. The liturgists do not go that far, but their statement leaves open that possibility by either ignoring or questioning traditional limits on deaconesses, while stressing the exclusive prerogative of bishops to make of deaconesses what they will.

We cannot, therefore, take seriously the liturgists' claim that "restoration of the female diaconate is such that neither doctrinal issues nor authoritative precedents are at stake." Neither can we accept their

---

[210] Alkiviadis Calivas and Philip Zymaris, "Ephesians 5:20–33 as the Epistle Reading for the Rite of Marriage: Appropriate or Problematic?" *Public Orthodoxy*, https://publicorthodoxy.org/2017/09/08/ephesians-rite-of-marriage/. Accessed Nov. 4, 2017.

assurances that deaconesses today will not lead to priestesses tomorrow, knowing where similar incremental innovations have led in heterodox communions. We also ought not to think only of what we ourselves might tolerate today. We must think generationally. Just as children who grow up in parishes with female readers are more likely to believe as adults that women should be deacons or deaconesses, so children who grow up in parishes with deaconesses will be more likely to believe as adults that women should be priests and bishops.

We therefore entreat all Orthodox hierarchs, other clergy, and theologians to uphold the dogmatic teaching of the Church concerning the creation and calling of man as male and female by resisting the divisive call to appoint deaconesses.

Signatories

Archimandrite Luke (Murianka), D.A. (Cand.)
Rector & Associate Professor of Patrology, Holy Trinity Orthodox Seminary (ROCOR)

Archpriest Chad Hatfield, D.Min., D.D.
President, St. Vladimir's Orthodox Theological Seminary (OCA)

Archpriest Alexander F.C. Webster, Ph.D.
Dean & Professor of Moral Theology, Holy Trinity Orthodox Seminary (ROCOR)

Protopresbyter George A. Alexson, Ph.D. (Cand.)
Holy Apostles Greek Orthodox Church (GOAA), Sterling, VA

Mitred Archpriest Victor Potapov
St. John the Baptist Russian Orthodox Cathedral (ROCOR), Washington, DC

Archimandrite Demetrios (Carellas)
Greek Orthodox Archdiocese of America (GOAA)

Archpriest A. James Bernstein
St. Paul Orthodox Church (AOCANA, Lynnwood, WA

Archpriest Lawrence Farley
St. Herman of Alaska Orthodox Church (OCA), Langley, BC

Archpriest Stephen Freeman
St. Anne Orthodox Church (OCA), Oak Ridge, TN

Archpriest Fr. Thaddaeus Hardenbrook
Saint Lawrence Orthodox Church (GOAA), Felton, CA

Archpriest Lawrence Margitich
St. Seraphim of Sarov Orthodox Church (OCA), Santa Rosa, CA

Archpriest Patrick Henry Reardon
All Saints Orthodox Church (AOCANA), Senior Editor, Touchstone, Chicago, IL

Archpriest Peter Heers, D.Th.
Assistant Professor of Old and New Testament, Holy Trinity Orthodox Seminary (ROCOR)

Archpriest Geoffrey Korz
All Saints of North America Orthodox Church (OCA), Hamilton Ontario

Archpriest Miroljub Srb. Ruzic
St. Nicholas the Wonderworker Orthodox Church (OCA), Center for Slavic and East European Studies, The Ohio State University, Columbus, OH

Archpriest David C. Straut
St. Elizabeth the New Martyr Orthodox Church (ROCOR), Rocky Hill, NJ

Archpriest John Whiteford
St. Jonah Orthodox Church (ROCOR), Spring, TX

Hieromonk Patrick (John) Ramsey, Ph.D.
(ROCOR) [On loan to the Metropolis of Limassol, Cyprus], Distance Tutor, Institute for Orthodox Christian Studies, Cambridge, England

Hieromonk Alexander (Reichert)
Acting Abbot, SS. Sergius & Herman of Valaam Monastery (ROCOR), Atlantic Mine, MI

Hieromonk Alexis Trader, D.Th.
Karakallou Monastery, Mt. Athos (Greece)

Fr. John E. Afendoulis
St. Spyridon Greek Orthodox Church (GOAA), Newport, RI

Fr. Kristian Akselberg, D.Phil. (Cand.)
St Andrew's Greek Orthodox Church (Ecumenical Patriarchate},
London, England

Fr. Christopher Allen
SS. Joachim and Anna Orthodox Church (ROCOR), San Antonio, TX

Fr. John Boddecker
SS. Theodore Orthodox Church (ROCOR), Buffalo, NY

Fr. Ignatius Green
Holy Virgin Protection Russian Orthodox Church (ROCOR), Nyack,
NY, Editor, St Vladimir's Seminary Press

Chaplain (Major) George Ruston Hill,
U.S. Army (OCA) Ethics Instructor, The Judge Advocate General's
Legal Center and School, Charlottesville, VA

Fr. Johannes Jacobse
St. Peter the Apostle Orthodox Church (AOCANA), Bonita Springs,
FL

Fr. Nathaniel Johnson
Saint Lawrence Orthodox Church (GOAA), Felton, CA

Fr. Andrew Kishler
St. George Antiochian Orthodox Church (AOCANA), Spring Valley,
IL

Fr. Seraphim Majmudar
Saint Nicholas Greek Orthodox Church (GOAA), Tacoma, WA

Chaplain (Captain) Christopher Moody
U.S. Army (GOAA) Fort Sill, OK

Fr. John A. Peck
All Saints of North America Orthodox Church (GOAA), Sun City, AZ

Fr. John Schmidt
(OCA-ROEA) St. Elias Orthodox Church, Ellwood City, PA

Fr. Gregory Telepneff, Th.D.
Senior Research Scholar, Center for Traditionalist Orthodox Studies

Protodeacon Jeremiah Davis
Greek Instructor, Orthodox Pastoral School in Chicago, Christ the Savior Orthodox Church (ROCOR), Wayne, WV

Protodeacon Brian Patrick Mitchell
St. John the Baptist Russian Orthodox Cathedral (ROCOR), Washington, DC

Deacon Nicholas Dujmovic, Ph.D.
Visiting Assistant Professor, Department of Politics, The Catholic University of America, Protection of the Holy Mother of God Orthodox Church (OCA-ROEA), Falls Church, VA

Deacon Stephen Hayes, D.Th.
Archdiocese of Johannesburg and Pretoria, Greek Orthodox Patriarchate of Alexandria and All Africa

Deacon Alexander William Laymon
Colonel, U.S. Army, Retired, St. Herman of Alaska Orthodox Church (ROCOR), Stafford, VA

Deacon Michael Pavuk
Director of Development, Holy Trinity Orthodox Seminary (ROCOR), Jordanville, NY

Deacon Ananias Sorem, Ph.D.
Lecturer in Philosophy, California State U. Fullerton, Falling Asleep of the Ever-Virgin Mary Church (OCA-ROEA), Anaheim, CA

Teena H. Blackburn
Lecturer in Philosophy and Religion, Eastern Kentucky University

David Bradshaw, Ph.D.
Professor of Philosophy, University of Kentucky

Mark J. Cherry, Ph.D.
Professor in Applied Ethics, Department of Philosophy, St. Edward's University

Corinna Delkeskamp-Hayes
Editor, Christian Bioethics, Freigericht, Germany

Tristram Engelhardt, Jr., Ph.D., M.D.
Professor, Rice University, Professor Emeritus, Baylor College of Medicine

Bruce V. Foltz, Ph.D.
Emeritus Professor of Philosophy, Eckerd College

David Ford, Ph.D.
Professor of Church History, St. Tikhon's Orthodox Theological Seminary (OCA)

Nancy Forderhase, Ph.D.
Emerita Professor of History, Eastern Kentucky University

Ana S. Iltis, Ph.D.
Professor of Philosophy, Director, Center for Bioethics, Health and Society, Wake Forest University

Nathan A. Jacobs, Ph.D.
Visiting Scholar of Philosophy, University of Kentucky, President, 5Sees Production Company

Joel Kalvesmaki, Ph.D.
Editor in Byzantine Studies, Dumbarton Oaks

James Kushiner
Executive Editor, Touchstone, Chicago, IL

George Michalopulos
Editor and Publisher, Monomakhos.com

Sampson (Ryan) Nash, MD, MA
Director, Ohio State University Center for Bioethics, Associate Professor of Medicine, Ohio State University College of Medicine

Alfred Kentigern Siewers, Ph.D.
Associate Professor of English, Bucknell University

Names of organizations are for identification only.

Bibliography

Primary Sources

Ambrose of Milan, *Enarratio in Psalmum 1*, PL 14, 921–952.

———, *On Virgins*, PL 16, 187–232.

Ambrosiaster, *Commentary on 1 Timothy*, PL 17, 461–481.

Apostolic Church Order (*Canones Ecclesiastici, Statutes of the Apostles*), trans. G. Horner (Oxford: Oxford University Press, 1915).

Apostolic Constitutions, ANF 7, 391–505.

Apostolic Tradition, trans. Alistair Stewart-Sykes (Crestwood, N.Y.: St. Vladimir's Seminary Press, 2001).

Basil the Great, Letter 188, PG 32, 664–684.

———, Letter 199, PG 32, 716–732.

———, *Moralia*, PG 31, 699–870.

———, Sermon 70, PG 31, 881–888, in *The Ascetic Works of Saint Basil*, trans. W.K.L. Clarke (London: Society for Promoting Christian Knowledge).

Balsamon, Theodore, *Responsa ad interrogationes Marci 35*, PG 138, 951–1012.

———, *Scholia in Concilium Chalcedonense*, PG 137, 381–502.

Blastares, Matthew, *Syntagma, littera Gamma*, PG 144, 1173–1176.

———, *Syntagma, littera Chi*, PG 145, 189–212.

The Canons of Hippolytus, ed. Paul Bradshaw, trans. Carol Bebawi (Nottingham: Grove Books Limited, 1987).

Clement of Alexandria, *Stromata*, PG 8.

Clement of Rome, *Epistle 1 to the Corinthians* (*1 Clement*), PG 1, 199–328.

Comnena, Anna, *Alexiad,* https://el.wikisource.org/wiki/Αλεξιάς/Βιβλίο_15, accessed August 20, 2016.

Cyprian of Carthage, Epistle 10, PL 4, 253–256.

———, Epistle 12, PL 4, 258–259.

———, Epistle 63, PL 4, 386A.

———, Epistle 73, Corpus Christianorum, *Series Latina*, III C, 529–562.

———, *On the Lapsed*, PL 4, 463–494.

Cyril of Jerusalem, *Procatechesis*, PG 33, 331–366.

De Jactantia Romanorum Levitarum (*On the Boastfulness of Roman Deacons*), PLS 3 3202.

Didascalia Apostolorum, trans. R.H. Connolly, Oxford, 1929.

Didascalia CCCXVIII Patrum Nicaenorum

Pseudo-Dionysius, *Celestial Hierarchy*, PG 3, 119–370.

———, *Divine Names*, PG 3, 586–996.

———, *Ecclesiastical Hierarchy*, PG 3, 370–584.

———, *Letter 8 to Demophilus*, PG 3, 1083–1100.

Epiphanius of Salamis, *Adversus Haereses*, PG 41–42; *The Panarion of Epiphanius of Salamis*, Vols. 1–2, trans. Frank Williams (New York: E.J. Brill, 1994).

Eusebius, *Ecclesiastical History*, PG 20 43–906.

Gregory the Great, Book 1, Epistles 19 and 20, PL 77, 464B–466A.

Gregory Nazianzus, Oration 8, PG 35, 789–817.

———, Oration 18, PG 35, 985–1044.

Hippolytus, *Refutation of All Heresies*, ANF 5, 9–153.

Ignatius, *Epistle to the Ephesians*, PG 5, 643–662.

———, *Epistle to the Magnesians*, PG 5, 662–674.

———, *Epistle to the Philadelphians*, PG 5, 698–708.

———, *Epistle to the Polycarp*, PG 5, 717–728.

———, *Epistle to the Smyrneans*, PG 5, 707–718.

———, *Epistle to the Trallians*, PG 5, 674–686.

Irenaeus of Lyon, *Adv. Her.*, PG 7, 427–1223.

———, Fragment 33, PG 7, 1245–1248.

Isidore of Pelusium, Epistle 1.90, PG 78 243–246.

Jerome, *Dialogus Adversus Pelagianos*, PL 23, 495–590.

——, Letter 127, PL 22, 1087–1095.

John Chrysostom, Homily 14 on Acts, PG 60, 111–120.

——, Homily 24 on Acts, PG 60, 183–192.

——, Homily 30 on Romans, PG 60, 661–668.

——, Homily 26 on 1 Corinthians, PG 61, 211–224.

——, Homily 34 on 1 Corinthians, PG 61, 285–296.

——, Homily 37 on 1 Corinthians, PG 61, 315–322.

——, Homily 9 on 1 Timothy, PG 62, 543–548.

——, Homily 11 on 1 Timothy, PG 62, 553–558.

Justin Martyr, *First Apology*, PG 6, 327–440.

Maximus the Confessor, Difficulty 41, PG 91, 1303–1314.

Pelagius, Commentary on 1 Corinthians, PLS 1, 1214.

——, Commentary on 1 Timothy, PLS 1, 1349.

——, Commentary on Titus, PLS 1, 1370.

Pliny the Younger, *Epistolae*, Book 10, Letter 96, in S.E. Stout, *Plinius, Epistolae: A Critical Edition* (Bloomington, Ill.: Indiana University Press, 1954), and Allen Cabaniss, *Pattern in Early Christian Worship* (Macon, Ga.: Mercer University Press, 1989).

Polycarp, Epistle to the *Philippians*, PG 5, 1096–1024.

The Shepherd of Hermas, PG 2, 891–1011.

Socrates, *Ecclesiastical History*, PG 67, 53–842.

Sozomen, *Ecclesiastical History*, PG 67, 843–1630.

Tertullian, *On the Veiling of Virgins*, PL 2, 887–914.

Testament of Our Lord (*Testamentum Domini*) trans. J. Cooper and A.J. Maclean, (Edinburgh, 1902).

Theodoret of Cyrus, Commentary on 1 Corinthians, PG 82, 337–348, in *Commentary on the Letters of St. Paul*, trans. Robert Charles Hill (Brookline, Mass.: Holy Cross Orthodox Press, 2001).

Secondary Sources

Balthasar, Hans Urs von, *Cosmic Liturgy: The Universe According to Maximus the Confessor*, trans. Brian E. Daly (San Francisco: Ignatius Press, 2003).

———, *The Glory of God: A Theological Aesthetic*, Vol. 2 (Edinburgh: T&T Clark, 1984).

Barnett, James Monroe, *The Diaconate: A Full and Equal Order* (New York: Seabury, 1981).

Behr-Sigel, Elisabeth *The Ministry of Women in the Church*, Steven Bigham trans. (Redondo Beach, Calif.: Oakwood Publiations, 1991).

Bradshaw, Paul F., *Ordination Rites of the Ancient Churches of East and West* (New York: Pueblo Publishing Company, 1990).

———, *The Search for the Origins of Christian Worship* (Oxford: Oxford University Press, second edition 2002).

Cabaniss, Allen, *Pattern in Early Christian Worship* (Macon, Ga.: Mercer University Press, 1989).

Chrissavgis, John, *Remembering and Reclaiming Diakonia: The Diaconate Yesterday and Today* (Brookline, Mass.: Holy Cross Orthodox Press, 2009).

Clark, Elizabeth A., *Women in the Early Church* (Collegeville, Minn.: The Liturgical Press, 1990).

Collins, John N., *Diakonia: Re-interpreting the Ancient Sources* (Oxford: Oxford University Press, 1990).

Connolly, R.H., *Didascalia Apostolorum* (Oxford: Oxford University Press, 1929).

Constas, Nicholas P. "Weaving the Body of God: Proclus of Constantinople, the Theotokos, and the Loom of the Flesh," *Journal of Early Christian Studies* 3 (1995) 169–194.

Costache, Doru, "Gender, Marriage, and Holiness in *Amb.Io.* 10 and 41" in Wendy Mayer and Ian J. Elmer, eds. *Men and Women in the Early Christian Centuries* (Strathfield, Australia: St Pauls Publications, 2014).

Cox, James J.C., *Note on the Title of the* Didascalia Apostolorum, *Andrews University Seminary Studies* (1975), 30–33.

Daniélou, Jean, *The Ministry of Women in the Early Church*, trans. Glyn Simon (London: The Faith Press, 1961).

Davies, J.G., "Deacons, Deaconesses, and the Minor Orders in the Patristic Period," *The Journal of Ecclesiastical History*, 14:1 (April 1963) 1–15.

Echlin, Edward P., *The Deacon in the Church, Past and Future* (New York: Society of St. Paul, 1971).

Eisen, Ute E., *Women Officeholders in Early Christianity: Epigraphical and Literary Studies*, trans. Linda M. Maloney (Collegeville, Minn.: Liturgical Press, 2000).

Elm, Susanna, *Virgins of God: The Making of Asceticism in Late Antiquity* (Oxford: Clarendon Press, 1994).

Ferguson, Everett, *The Early Church at Work and Worship: Volume I: Ministry, Ordination, Covenant, and Canon* (Eugene, Ore: Cascade Books, 2013).

FitzGerald, Kyriaki Karidoyanes, *Women Deacons in the Orthodox Church: Called to Holiness and Ministry* (Brookline, Mass.: Holy Cross Orthodox Press, 1999).

Gryson, Roger, *The Ministry of Women in the Early Church*, trans. Jean Laporte et al. (Collegeville, Minn.: The Liturgical Press, 1976), originally published as *Le ministère des femmes dans l'Église ancienne* (Gembloux, Belgium: Éditions J. Duculot, 1972).

Gvosdev, Ellen, *The Female Diaconate: An Historical Perspective* (Minneapolis, Minn.: Light and Life, 1991).

Holum, Kenneth G., *Theodosian Empresses: Women and Imperial Dominion in Late Antiquity* (Berkeley: University of California Press, 1982).

Hopko, Thomas, ed., *Women and the Priesthood* (Crestwood, N.Y.: St. Vladimir's Seminary Press, 1999).

Karras, Valerie A., "Female Deacons in the Byzantine Church," *Church History*, 73:2 (June 2004) 272–316.

———, "The Liturgical Function of Consecrated Women in the Byzantine Church," *Theological Studies*, 66 (2005) 96–116.

———, "Orthodox Theologies of Women and Ordained Ministry," *Thinking Through Faith: New Perspectives from Orthodox Christian Scholars*, eds. A. Papanikolaou, E. Prodromou (Crestwood, NY: St. Vladimir's Seminary Press, 2008), 113–158.

Kennedy, B. David, "Diaconate in the Ukrainian Catholic Church," *Chrysostom*, 7, No. 1 (Spring, 1985) 9–15.

Louth, Andrew, *Denys the Areopagite* (Wilton, Conn.: Morehouse-Barlow, 1989).

Mainoldi, Ernesto Sergio, "Why Dionysius the Areopagite? The Invention of the First Father." In *Studia Patristica Vol. XCVI*, edited by Markus Vinzent, 425–40. Leuven: Peeters, 2017.

Martimort, Aimé Georges, *Deaconesses: An Historical Study*, trans. K.D. Whitehead (San Francisco: Ignatius Press, 1986).

Marucci, Corrado, "Il 'diaconato' di Febe (*Rom*. 16,1–2) secondo l'esegesi moderna," *Diakonia, Diaconiae, Diaconato, Semantica e Storia nei padri della Chiesa* (Roma: Institutum Patristicum Augustinianum, 2010), republished in English as "The 'Diaconate' of Phoebe (Rom. 16:1–2) According to Modern Exegesis," *Women Deacons: Essays with Answers*, ed. Phyllis Zagano (Collegeville, Minn.: Liturgical Press, 2016), 1–12.

Mitchell, Brian Patrick, "The Problem with Hierarchy: Ordered Relations in God and Man," *St. Vladimir's Theological Quarterly*, 54:2 (2010) 189–217.

Mitchell, Patrick, *The Scandal of Gender: Early Christian Teaching on the Man and the Woman* (Salisbury, Mass.: Regina Orthodox Press, 1998).

Nikolaou, Stefano, "A Survey of Byzantine Responses to Islam," unpublished dissertation, Australian Catholic University, 2007, http://www.answering-islam.org/history/byzantine_responses.html, accessed August 23, 2016.

Ostrogorsky, George, *History of the Byzantine State* (New Brunswick, N.J.: Rutgers University Press, 1969).

Perl, Eric D., *Theophany: The Neoplatonic Philosophy of Dionysius the Areopagite* (Albany, N.Y.: State University of New York Press, 2007).

Pothan, Peter S.C., "The Subjection of the Laity," *Religion and Society*, 55, 1–2 (March-June) 2010, 36–46.

Quasten, Johannes, *Music & Worship in Pagan & Christian Antiquity*, trans. Boniface Ramsey (Washington, DC: National Association of Pastoral Musicians, 1983; originally published as *Musik und Gesang in den Kulten der heidnischen Antike und christlichen Fruhzeit*, by Aschendorff, Munster, Germany, 1973).

———, *Patrology*, Vol. I–IV (Westminster, Md.: Christian Classics, Inc., 1983; originally published in English by SPECTRUM Press, Utrecht, Holland, 1950).

Ramsey, John, *The Minor Clergy of the Orthodox Church: Their Role and Life according to the Canons* (John Ramsey, 2016).

Reynolds, Roger E., "An Early Medieval Tract on the Diaconate," *The Harvard Theological Review*, 72, 1–2 (January-April 1979) 97–100.

Sorci, Pietro, "Diaconato e altri ministeri liturgici della donna," *La Donna nel pensiero cristiano antico*, ed. Umberto Mattioli (Genova: Marietti Editore, 1992), 331–361, republished in English as "The Diaconate and Other Liturgical Ministries of Women," *Women Deacons: Essays with Answers*, ed. Phyllis Zagano (Collegeville, Minn.: Liturgical Press, 2016), 57–95.

Steinhauser, Kenneth B., "Authority in the Primitive Church," *The Patristics and Byzantine Reivew*, 3, 1–2 (1984) 89–100.

Stiefel, Jennifer H., "Women Deacons in 1 Timothy: A Linguistic and Literary Look at 'Women Likewise ...' (1 Tim. 3:11)," *New Testament Studies* 41 (1995) 442–457.

Stout, S.E., *Plinius, Epistolae, a Critical Edition*, (Bloomington, Ind.: Indiana University Press, 1962)

Sutherland, K., and P. Allen, "Many Gifts: One Form of Service," *New Blackfriars*, 58, 684 (May 1977) 214–219.

Taft, Robert F., 'Women at Church in Byzantium: Where, When—and Why?' *Dumbarton Oaks Papers*, 52 (1998) 27–87.

Theodorou, Evangelos, "The Institution of Deaconesses in the Orthodox Church and the Possibility of Its Restoration," *The Place of the Woman in the Orthodox Church and the Question of the Ordination of Women: InterOrthodox Symposium, Rhodos, Greece, 30 October–7 November 1988*, ed. Gennadios Limouris (Katerini, Greece: Tertios Publications, 1992), 207–238.

———, "Service of God and Service of Man," *Theologia*, 68:3 (July-September 1997) 417–431.

Topping, Eva Catafygiotu, *Sacred Songs: Studies in Byzantine Hymnography* (Minneapolis, Minn.: Light & Life Publishing, 1997).

Vagaggini, Cipriano, "La diaconessa nella tradizione greca e bizantina," *Il Regno* 32 (1987) 672–673, republished in English as "The Deaconess in the Byzantine Tradition," *Women Deacons: Essays with*

Answers, ed. Phyllis Zagano (Collegeville, Minn.: Liturgical Press, 2016), 96–99.

———, "L'ordinazione delle diaconesse nella tradizione greca e bizantina," *Orentialia christiana periodica* 40 (1974) 146–189, republished in English as "The Ordination of Deaconesses in the Greek and Byzantine Tradition," *Women Deacons: Essays with Answers*, ed. Phyllis Zagano (Collegeville, Minn.: Liturgical Press, 2016), 100–143.

Van Zyl, Hermie C., "The Evolution of Church Leadership in the New Testament: A New Consensus," *Neotestamentica* 32, 2 (1998) 585–604.

Viscuso, Patrick Demetrios, *Sexuality, Marriage, and Celibacy in Byzantine Law: The Alphabetical Collection of Matthew Blastares* (Brookline, Mass.: Holy Cross Orthodox Press, 2008).

Wijngaards, John, *Women Deacons in the Early Church: Historical Texts and Contemporary Debate* (New York: Crossroad Publishing, 2002).

Witherington, Ben, *Women in the Earliest Churches* (Cambridge: Cambridge University Press, 1988).

Wybrew, Hugh, *Orthodox Feasts of Jesus Christ and the Virgin Mary* (Crestwood, N.Y.: St. Vladimir Seminary Press, 2000).

Zanetti, Ugo, "Y eut-il des diaconesses en Égypte?" *Vetera Christianorum* 27 (1990) 369–73, republished in English as "Were There Deaconesses in Egypt?" *Women Deacons: Essays with Answers*, ed. Phyllis Zagano (Collegeville, Minn.: Liturgical Press, 2016), 100–143.

About the Author

BRIAN PATRICK MITCHELL holds a PhD in theology and an MTh in Orthodox studies from the University of Winchester and a BA in English literature from the University of Cincinnati. He is a protodeacon of the Russian Orthodox Church Abroad, a former soldier and cabinet-level speechwriter, a former Washington bureau chief of *Investor's Business Daily*, and the author of several books and many articles on politics and religion, including an epic historical romance entitled *A Crown of Life* and an innovative work of political of theory entitled *Eight Ways to Run the Country*, which has been used to teach politics at Yale and elsewhere. His doctoral dissertation, entitled *Origen's Revenge: The Greek and Hebrew Roots of Christian Thinking on Male and Female*, will be published later in 2021 by Pickwick Publications, an imprint of Wipf and Stock. He and his wife have three grown children, all married and all faithful Orthodox Christians. His personal blog is brianpatrickmitchell.com.

Index

M

Macrina the Younger, St., 20
Mainoldi, Ernesto Sergio, 63,92
Marcella of Rome, St., 50
Marcionites, 48
Mark III (patriarch of
   Alexandria), 33,39
Martimort, Aimé Georges, 6-7,
   10, 17-18, 20-36, 39-40, 47, 78,
   92
Marucci, Corrado, 8,10,42,92
Mary Magdalene, St., 13-14,57
Maximus the Confessor, St., 23,
   51, 89, 90
Michael the Great, 35
Mitchell, Brian Patrick, 51,71,78,
   85, 92, 97
Montanists, 29-30,44-45,48,51
Myrrhbearers, 33,47,70

N

Nectarius, St. (archbishop of
   Constantinople), 20
Neoplatonism, 63
Nestorius (archbishop of
   Constantinople), 36,69
Nicephorus I (emperor), 38
Nikolaou, Stefano, 39,92
Nina of Georgia, St., 57
nuns, 3, 24, 28, 30, 33, 47, 70, 78-
   79

O

Olga, St. (princess of Russia), 57
Olympias, St. (deaconess), 20-21,
   24
Origen, xii, 7, 44, 51, 63, 97

Ostrogorsky, Georges, 38,92

P

Patriarchate of Alexandria, xi,xii,
   77, 85
Paul of Samosata, 18
Paul, St., the Apostle, 6-9,14,27,
   38, 41, 43, 45, 49-50, 54-56, 64,
   74, 80
   on diverse gifts and offices, 54-
      56
   on head-covering, 43
   on silence, 43,49,50
   on St. Phoebe, 6
   on subjection, 50
   on widows, 20
   use of *diakonos*, 6, 55
Paulianists, 18-19,48,68
Pelagians, 47
Pelagius, 45,61,89
Philip, St., the Evangelist, 43-44,
   58
Phoebe of Cenchrea, St., xii,6-8,
   10, 15, 52, 57, 67-68, 71, 74, 92
Photine the Samaritan, St., 57
Photius, St. (archbishop of
   Constantinople), 31
Platonida of Nisibis, St., 17
Pliny the Younger, 9, 89
Polycarp of Smyrna, St., 9-10,58,
   88-89
Pothan, Peter S.C., 56,92
presbyters, 11, 13-16, 18-19, 51,
   55-56, 58, 60-63, 67, 69
presbytides/female presidents,
   52, 62
priesthood, 19,22,25,29,63
Priscilla, St. (wife of Aquila), 56
prophesying, 43-44

prophetesses, 15,44
Protoevangelium of James, 41
Pseudo-Dionysius, 63-65
Pseudo-Dionysius, 23,27,63-65, 88
Pulcheria, St. (empress), 36,69

Q

Quasten, Johannes, 12,14,32,37, 47-48, 59, 92
Quintillianists, 51

R

Radegunde of Poitiers, St., 30
Ramsey, Patrick (John), 27,83,93
readers, 15-16,19,21-22,26,29, 47, 59, 70, 75-76, 78, 82
ritual purity, 35,39,42
Romanides, John, 37

S

Seven, the (deacons), 58,60-61
Seventy Apostles, 56,58
Severus of Antioch, 23,28,75
silence, 44,49-50
singers, 15,33,46
  See also chanters
singing, 16,18,33,36,46-49,70
  See also chanting
singing vs. chanting, 46
Sorci, Pietro, 12,18,52-53,93
Sozomen, 20-21,89
Stephen, St., the Protomartyr, 15, 29,57,61
Stiefel, Jennifer H., 10,93
Stout, S.E., 9,89,93
subdeaconesses, 47

subdeacons, 3,15-16,19,21-22, 26,28-29, 47, 59, 70, 75, 78
subjection, 2,50-51,70,73-74,76
Sutherland, K., 58,93

T

Taft, Robert F., 16,23,93
Tertullian, 29,38,62,64,89
Testament of Our Lord Jesus Christ, 11,16
The Shepherd of Hermas, 55,60, 89
Thecla of Iconium, St., 57
Theodoret of Cyrus, 45,73,89
Theodorou, Evangelos, 17,26-27, 77,93
Theodosius the Great, St. (emperor), 20-21,80
Theotokos, the, 19,27,41,69,81, 90
Timothy of Alexandria, St., 39,41
Topping, Eva Catafygiotu, 47,93

V

Vagaggini, Cipriano, 18-19,26,93
Vigilius of Rome (pope), 61
virgins, 2, 14-15,20,22-23,30,37, 42,47,49, 69
Viscuso, Patrick, 40,65,94

W

White Monastery, 31
widows, 2,14-16,20-23,29-30, 32,42,52,57,59-60,78-80
wives, 7-8, 10,21-22,28,30-31, 36,68, 79
Wybrew, Hugh, 41,94

Y

Z

Printed in the USA
CPSIA information can be obtained
at www.ICGtesting.com
LVHW020230240124
769826LV00003B/14